DARK DEATHS

FÉLIX J. FOJO

UNOS & OTROS
EDICIONES

Copyright © 2018 Félix Fojo

All rights reserved.

Title: Dark Deaths

Author: Félix Fojo

Edition: Armando Nuviola

Cover desigh by: Armando Nuviola

Copyright © 2018 All rights reserved.

ISBN: 10: 0-9998707-3-4

ISBN-13: 978-0-9998707-3-0

UNOS & OTROS
EDICIONES

All rigths reserved. No part of this publication may be reproduced, stored in a retrieval system, or transmitted, in any form, or by any means without the prior written permission of the publisher.

infoeditorialunosotros@gmail.com
www.unosotrosculturalproject.com

Made in USA, 2018

DARK DEATHS

FÉLIX J. FOJO

Copyright © 2018 Félix Fojo

All rights reserved.

Title: Dark Deaths

Author: Félix Fojo

Edition: Armando Nuviola

Cover desigh by: Armando Nuviola

Copyright © 2018 All rights reserved.

ISBN: 10: 0-9998707-3-4

ISBN-13: 978-0-9998707-3-0

All rigths reserved. No part of this publication may be reproduced, stored in a retrieval system, or transmitted, in any form, or by any means without the prior written permission of the publisher.

infoeditorialunosotros@gmail.com
www.unosotrosculturalproject.com

Made in USA, 2018

INDEX

INTRODUCTION 7

EDGARD ALLAN POE. BRIEF CLINICAL HISTORY ..11

SUICIDE AND POETRY............................21

YES! I JUST KILLED JOHN LENNON!..........................31

THE STRANGE DEATH OF JULIÁN DEL CASAL.......40

DID OSCAR WILDE DIE OF SORROW? 46

FROM WHAT DID THE LITTLE GIRL OF GUATEMALA ACTUALLY DIE?......................................52

A CURSED MOVIE 62

WHAT KILLED PRESIDENT GARFIELD? 66

TO DIE YOUNG 75

DARK DEATHS 87

Introduction

Let's start to enter the subject, by narrating some details of a case of which I had reliable references, even written, and that served for the colleagues who were leaving me alerted about the healthy doubt that all medical professionals must have before the death, any death, especially when we are the ones who must certify their causes clinically and legally.

While doing the rural medical service in Oriente Province, Cuba, in the 70s, I learned about the case of an old man who had died several years earlier in my work area, around 1964 or 1965, apparently of cerebral hemorrhage. The truth is that a young and inexperienced doctor, like almost all of us at that time, had issued, after a brief physical examination of the corpse, without carrying out an autopsy because it was not considered necessary, the corresponding death certificate corroborating this diagnosis.

Well, when unleashed a disagreeable family dispute after a few plots of land, a modest house, some cash and animals, all inheritable inheritance of the old man, the problem escalated to the extreme of taking action on the matter the police and decree the prosecution an exhumation of the body of the deceased. And yes, in fact, once the legal order was carried out, the cerebral hemorrhage, which must have been very abundant, was confirmed as the cause of death, but not produced by an atherosclerotic vascular accident as it was believed and how it had been legally certified. but by a line nail, a railroad pole about ten centimeters long that penetrated the occipital region (covered the flat head of the metal object by the abundant hair of the neck) and remained, as an accusing witness, inside the skull of the deceased .

That, without a doubt, had once been an unthinkable, obscure death, actually a murder, although the innocent doctor who filled the initial certificate of death did not even think of such an event.

Why? Because in his inexperienced youthful candor he believed what he saw superficially and what they told him: Man in the third age with years of suffering from recognized and well documented chronic diseases, among them arterial hypertension, a respectable peasant family composed of healthy people dedicated to the hard work, a rustic but friendly and socially recognized environment, an explicit family harmony apparently seamless, in short, the ideal ... to make mistakes and screw up.

And deaths like that, dark, strange, suspicious, without clear and definite explanations, or with many possible contradictory explanations, not concordant, anomalous, is full of the hazardous history of medicine that is nothing more than the history of humanity.

Of course we are not implying that everyone dies murdered, no, and less with an iron nail inside the head, but what we are reasonably sure, after a fairly extensive medical experience and reading history, good story for many years, is that many causes of death, especially in powerful and / or famous people, but also in ordinary mortals of the bunch, deserve, in the name of historical justice and a reasonable approach to the truth, a new and closer look .

We do not intend to do in this simple volume paleopathography, that relatively new forensic specialty that studies in situ, and with advanced technology, bones, mummies and tombs in order to diagnose, as would be done in an ultramodern hospital, the most recondite diseases and causes of death of the deceased that lie under the microscopes and magnetic resonance devices.

Our expectations are much more modest but they are fed by the same enthusiasm to go a little further in the diagnosis, the medical key par excellence, to offer a new vision of certain terminal events, to deepen, with the scalpel of clinical logic and common sense, in some topics, narrations of facts that are repeated again and again and not always conform to rational thinking. We do not aspire, that is obvious, to find nails of line in all the skulls; we are satisfied that the reader finds, once in a while, a detail or a possible explanation that has been overlooked previously or that could tempt a budding researcher to a more detailed historical investigation.

But if all this is very complicated, we feel satisfied then to tell our readers some new historical facet, reveal the final episodes of certain characters that have gone unnoticed and above all, and I think is the most important, entertain, legitimate end and last of the literature.

We invite you then to a trip through somewhat macabre and somber places, it is true, but at the end of the day interesting.

We aspire to enjoy it.

>The author

Edgard Allan Poe. Brief clinical history

Only forty years.

Yes, believe it or not, the American Edgar Allan Poe, journalist, editor, poet, story teller, novelist and essayist, the father of the crime novel, of symbolism, of the so-called dark romanticism, and to some extent of the American Gothic and Science Fiction, one of the most influential literary personalities of the last two centuries, barely lived forty years, from january 19th, 1809 to october 7th, 1849.

And let us not be surprised, my reading friend, the work of Poe, that master of the rationalization of the irrational, portrays and announces death in all its forms and manifestations: natural, premeditated, mysterious, accidental, misleading, placid, truculent, imagined, dreamed, wanted, rejected. Poe had an obsession with death, no matter whether friend or foe, who announces and fulfills its early destiny. A trait that, I don't know if it has been pointed out earlier, relates him to another early dead, the Cuban José Martí, who, incidentally, left unfinished the Spanish translation of Poe's poem *Annabel Lee,* but that is a story that doesn't belong here.

The surprising thing is that a man who actually began to do full-time literature at 27 (At 18 he published a small book of poems, *Tamerlane and Other Poems*; and from 22 or 23 did some journalism), and so he had only thirteen years to develop it, marked so profoundly so many writers, painters, musicians and even much later, filmmakers: Baudelaire and Rimbaud, Robert Louis Stevenson and H.P. Lovecraft, Conan Doyle and Mark Twain, Oscar Wilde and Jules Verne, Dostoyevsky and Valdimir Nabokov, Mallarmé and Rubén Darío, Andrés Caicedo and Julián del Casal, Wilkie Collins and Agatha Christie, Cortázar and Jorge Luis Borges, Ray Bradbury and Stephen King, Manet and Matisse, D.W. Griffith and Roger Corman, Federico Fellini and Alfred Hitchcock, Lou Reed and David Bowie, Debussy and Ravel, and many, many more who openly acknowledge and thank him or who don't mention and hide him, doesn't matter.

As expressed in a poem dedicated to Poe the Argentinian Jorge Luis Borges:

Perhaps, on the other side of death, he continues to erect, solitary and strong, splendid and atrocious wonders.

More surprising, however, is the knowledge that in that short life Poe suffered major health burns and addictions, including alcohol, opium, and gambling, as well as the abrupt loss of several women he loved, also in an addictive way, including among them the image of his mother (he didn't really knew her, she died when he was two years old) and his extremely young wife, and also niece Virginia Clemm, whom he married when she was thirteen years old, this facts conspired, or perhaps favored, against his literary productivity.

Let's try then, it may be interesting, to establish a brief clinical history of the hypothetical "patient Poe", knowing in advance that the diagnosis of symptoms and clinical signs in the writer's health hardships is complicated by the fact that he had very aggressive enemies, perhaps the proper adjective would be envious, they negam to roll up blunders, exaggerations and misrepresentations about the social and physical difficulties of the man, which has brought about all kinds of confusion in the attempt to biograph and pathograph Poe.

An anecdote illustrates our statement. On one occasion, one of many, he was accused of having plagiarized the German writer E.T.A. Hoffmann, who had worked a little before Poe on a horror story: «Horror (stories) come from Germany», they said to him, and Poe, who wasn't very good at defending himself, but did own an exquisite sensitivity, replied: "Horror comes from the soul".

And to top it off, the "friend" and self-titled executor of Poe, the mediocre and proven counterfeiter R.W. Griswold, appropriated his papers and wrote, two years after the death of the poet, a preface to his complete works and a biography that have gone down in history as one of the most perfidious and slanderous documents ever written about a first class literary person. The so-called *Griswold Memory* disrupted the public perception of Edgard Allan Poe for more than a century, and even today some of his assertions continue to be repeated without serious criticism.

The clarification is important because many of Poe's real or supposed antisocial attitudes we know through the filter of these people. There is no doubt that the writer had problems, behavioral oddities, addictions, diseases, even some attitudes that may have bordered sociopathy, but the true magnitude of these manifestations must be taken with tweezers.

That said, let's review the more or less confirmed anamnesis of this artistic genius.

Poe, after a lonely and unhappy childhood brought on by the premature death of their parents, but with the luck to live a realeased adolescence thanks to their adoption relatives, Frances and John Allan, who gave him education, surname and offered him a home, began drinking at just seventeen years of age. At the same time he manifested mood swings that ranged from depression to euphoria. Poe himself described them in a letter to a friend:

I have such marked changes, from the greatest persistent depression I can pass to immense exaltation or jubilation with a great voracity to work.

A rather obvious bipolar condition that couldn't be diagnosed at that time because it hadn't yet been described. His alcoholism was sporadic, but intense. His years in the military were very good from the point of view of his mental stability but his attempt to study at the university didn't end well, among other things due to gambling debts and the (definitive) fight with his adoptive father, a dispute that left him without funds and forced him to write some mercenary works.

It should be noted that Poe's alcoholism was very *sui generis,* only one or two drinks were enough for his personality and behavior to deteriorate rapidly. Today we know that in some people there is a congenital deficiency of a liver enzyme, Alcohol Dehydrogenase (ADH), which, when absent, greatly increases the toxic effects of alcohol. It's possible that Poe may have suffered from this not very common condition (researcher Arno Karlen's theory), but we have no way of knowing for sure. At any rate, he relapsed frequently into drinking, knowing the disastrous effects he would have to deal with later. It's very significant this autobiographical fragment of the writer:

As an insult, my enemies attributed my madness to alcohol instead of alcohol abuse to madness.

Is it possible that Poe confused with madness what was only a genetic condition? It's perfectly possible, but the addiction was there. However, his problems didn't end with alcohol.

In 1999, neurology professor C. Bazil (neurologists Weissberg, Zumbach and Ingram, in different works, agree with this diagnosis) postulated the possibility that Poe was a carrier of a temporal lobe epilepsy of the brain brought upon, or not, by the consumption of alcohol. This neurological disease would explain the confusion so common in Poe, the psychomotor automatisms (strange movements with hands, grimaces and dreams) that many of his contemporaries refer to seeing in him (or narrated by himself) and the absence of convulsions.

This type of epilepsy, called Jacksonian epilepsy, was not described until about forty years after Poe's death by neurologist John H. Jackson. In some patients with Jacksonian epilepsy, the development of larval psychosis (postictal psychosis) has been confirmed, which could explain, if so, the deterioration of Poe's psyche in the last months of his life.

A doctor who treated Poe's wife and nurse Maria Luisa Shew (whom Poe tried her to fall in love with him after his wife's death), a friend of the marriage, describe facial asymmetries «and a rare weakness in the face» of the writer , signs that may coincide with temporal lobe epilepsy. It is suggestive to point out that Poe, who wasn't a physician, describes very well epileptic seizures with hallucinations in several of his stories. The small cranial traumatisms repeated in the course of his drunkenness and confusion, including, of course, the much more serious one that seems to have killed him, have not been ruled out as the cause of the writer's neurological problems.

In the last months of his life, the confused state that Poe sometimes presented, becomes more frequent, is aggravated, and some of his contemporaries refer to having witnessed in him fabulous and expressed thoughts that bordered the delirious in the course of conversations and discussions. In periods of exaltation or under the influence of alcohol, Poe became very loquacious, exuberant, sometimes verbose, and that symptom seems to be exacerbated in this final stage.

Let's talk about Poe's controversial physical end.

Edgar Allan Poe's death is one of the most commented tragic episodes of modern literature. In fact, twenty different versions (we have found 22) of the causes and facts related to that death have been postulated, but at least all agree with the place of his death, George Washington College Hospital in Baltimore, Maryland.

Let's try to reconstruct the facts. 1849 was a particularly complicated year (weren't the previous ones too?) for Poe: He had gotten into his head, once again, to establish a literary magazine but didn't have the funds to run such a company; he was in love with a stubbornness with an old love from his adolescence (Sarah Elmira Royster) but at the same time had become entangled with Helen Whitman and probably also with Annie Richmond, sentimental situations that he carried with little skill, which caused him great anxiety. Supposedly he was trying to quit drinking (his difficult girlfriends demanded it), which may have made him even more nervous and irritable.

Now the final events.

There are several witnesses that claimed that Poe suffered a confusional crisis in the train in which he traveled to Philadelphia to give a conference (the editor John Sartain was one of those witnesses), but couldn't do it, couldn't control hid thoughts properly, and decided to return to New York.

This is where everything gets confused as Poe actually appeared in Baltimore, a city where he was found several days later wandering the streets, or in a tavern (the tavern existed, it was called Gunner's Hall and was at 44 East Lombard St.), there is no definite agreement on that. The truth is that he was dressed in ragged clothes and a straw hat that were not his and was in an shabby and incoherent condition. Some acquaintances rescue him and he is taken to the hospital. Mr. Soundgrass, known to Poe and one of those who lead him to the health center (Baltimore journalist Joseph P. Walker was the other), claims that the writer was in poor physical condition "he was hard to look at", he said, but still conscious.

Dr. Moran, the doctor that recieves him at the hospital, diagnosed him with delirium tremens (an alcoholic intoxication) but at the same time writes that he didn't have ethylic breath and refused to having drink alcohol (we are in 1849 and doctors also thought, logically, in a deprivation crisis). In a few hours he falls into a coma and dies two and a half days later. The case was closed as a liver crisis due to customary alcoholism and a "brain inflammation", a very common term at that time to refer to deaths of causes not well defined but generally related to drunkenness and tavern fights.

An autopsy was not performed, which leaves us blind about the poet's organic state (especially the liver and brain).

The truth is that Poe wasn't drunk at the time of his hospital admission and so is stated in the reference written by Dr. Moran. He states very clearly that the patient had no ethylic breath or alcohol odor in his clothes. What tragic situation brought him there and subsequently to death? Let us briefly review some of the many hypotheses that have been shuffled over and over again.

1. Was Poe murdered to rob him? Poe was penniless and probably didn't carry anything of value. His economic invalidity was widely known. He didn't have penetrating wounds of importance if we were to believe Dr. Moran.

2. Was he drugged by the vote hunters, there were elections in Baltimore on those days, and things like that often happened, and then abandoned in a tavern (the cooping theory)? Much has been discussed about this and I have no elements to confirm or deny it. It may have happened and is one of the most popular theories to explain the facts.

3. Was it really a hepatic coma? Dr. Moran appeared to have been a well-trained physician and doesn't refer in his examination jaundice or the typical breath of these patients (hepatic foetor).

4. Did he suffer a severe fall or blow of a criminal nature in the head and developed a subarachnoid hemorrhage? It is a diagnosis that seems very probable and explains the progressive deterioration of the patient's condition, ending in deep coma and death. In my opinion, it is the picture that comes closest to the (narrated) symptomatology of the patient.

5. Was it the accelerated deterioration of his epileptic condition that killed him? It's possible, considering that at that time there was no such diagnosis, much less an appropriate treatment. Today, a Jacksonian epilepsy ending in death is very rare, unusual, but not at that time.

6. Apoplexy? Poe was still walking when he was rescued and no sign of focus was noted in Dr. Moran's examination. Such an event seems extremely improbable.

7. A brain tumor? Brain neoplasms sometimes produ-

ce very erratic symptoms, but it is difficult for them to explain Poe's neurological condition for so long. Here we miss the absence of an autopsy.

8. Suicide? An obscure incident occurred a year earlier, apparently related to an overdose of laudanum (legal at that time). But this time the symptomatology doesn't correspond and much less the outcome.

9. Was Poe tuberculous and hid it? It could be, but no symptoms and signs of such illness have been reported, although his wife did die tuberculous. His way of dying doesn't correspond to this disease.

10. Pneumonia? There are endless things that this diagnosis doesn't take into account. The symptomatology doesn't correspond either (Absence of cough, fever, sputum, shortness of breath).

11. Hypoglycemic crisis? The symptomatology doesn't correspond and it has never been proven that Poe was diabetic.

12. Syphilis? Although he may have suffered it, occasions of contagion he certainly had, tertiary syphilis presents other very different neurological signs.

13. Poisoning by heavy metals, especially mercury? It is an interesting hypothesis, but there is a report, a sample of hair taken many years later, that seems to deny the fact.

14. Cholera? No one has mentioned diarrhea among the signs that Poe presented.

15. Did a stray dog bite him and died of rabies? Symptoms don't correspond and no lesions of this type were described.

16. Carbon monoxide poisoning? It seems to us an absurd theory.

On this path, as we have already mentioned, more than twenty possible causes of death have been raised, some even far-fetched or unequivocally ridiculous.

We have to give up to the fact that we will never know the truth, but whatever it was, that October day one of the most important literary minds in history was gone. A higher mind from the point of view of literary creation that due to its other weaknesses must also carry a true black legend.

Jorge Luis Borges, one of the few who really studied Poe, wrote referring to the writer's final hours:

> In his delirium he repeated the words he had put in the mouth of a sailor who died, in one of his earliest accounts, on the edge of the South Pole. In 1849, the sailor and he died at one time. Those words were: This is the knell of death.
>
> It's a beautiful phrase, Borges was a master at that, but it doesn't seem to correspond with reality.
>
> With Poe dead, and with the pain of not having unraveled the physical causes of his

death, let us close this brief essay with the opinion of the French poet Charles Baudelaire, almost certainly the man who introduced Edgard Allan Poe and made him known in Europe, even before North America itself:

There are in the history of literature destinies of men who carry the word 'fatality' written in mysterious characters in the sinuous folds of the forehead, such was the case of Poe, the most original, the most sensitive and the most unfortunate of the poets.

A worthy epitaph.

Suicide and poetry

Why do poets kill themselves so often?

Suicide, the act of ending one's own life, is considered a grave sin by almost all monotheistic religions, and some polytheists, and a serious crime by the jurisprudence of various countries.

For some, suicide is an act of cowardice and for others an action of supreme courage. For us, those who practice medicine, is a sign of maladjustment, outburst or mental illness, except, of course, that there is a cause that makes it practically imperative, but that is something extremely rare.

And it is also, as the Argentinian writer Horacio Gonzalez says: "The non-desire for life and to judge oneself as not deserving to continue enjoying it, implies a special kind of guilt or acceptance of the highest price that is paid to send the posthumous relief or compensation message".

Relief to whom, to compensate what? We ask. Or, as the French writer and Nobel laureate Albert Camus postulated: "There is only one truly serious philosophical problem: suicide" (*The Myth of Sisyphus*, 1942). A statement that points directly to the ultimate meaning of life.

The truth is that the suicidal act, as the psychoanalyst Silvia Tubert tells us, snatches the subject whose speech is the only one that would give us access to its understanding. In short, a theme, without a doubt, complex and changing, nuanced in our days by new legal, moral and even political approaches. But, leaving aside the old and always renewed philosophical, moral and ethical debate. Why is suicide so common among poets of all generations? It is enough to review the history of literature to realize that the prevalence of this phenomenon is very high among the cultivators of the above artistic genre, and not now, but always:

"There is only one truly serious philosophical problem: suicide".

An example: The greek Sappho of Mytilene or of Lesbos (? - 580 BCE), one of the nine great cultivators of the lyric genre in the golden age Greece, threw herself into the sea from the dark rock of Léucade by the love of a woman (Or was it from a man, the navigator Phaon):

I really want to die / That one left me, crying / and on leaving said / Oh Sappho, what terrible pain ours! / Without me wanting it I'm leaving you.

The suicidal act, as a final decision, egoistic or altruistic according to the case, of any subject, has existed, as we said above, forever, what has changed through history is the attitude of society towards this act. Greeks and Romans didn't regard suicide badly, as long as it was worthily executed (the use of rope, for example, which left the corpse floating inert between heaven and earth, was deplorable). Even Plato recommended calling death when life became "immoderate" because of great suffering. But the fathers of the Church, St. Augustine of Hippo (4th century) and then St. Thomas Aquinas (13th century) forced suicide into the world of sin, of mortal sin, a kind of double suicide: body and soul, based on the fifth commandment: "Thou shalt not kill" and thus modifying to this day the social perception of the act. The Church was so committed to the suicide act that the Councils of Braga (562) and Toledo (693) denied the burial on consecrated land, and those who attempted it, even without success, condemned them to excommunication, a penalty that today seems to be ridiculous, but it was truly frightening in those dark times.

Let's get back to the suicidal poets. It is at the end of the eighteenth century and the beginning of the nineteenth, the time of the awakening of Romanticism, when the true epidemic of suicide among poets begins.

Let us know a few: The promising English Bard Thomas Chatterton kills himself by ingesting arsenic, a dreadful death, at only seventeen years of age: *"To exist is not to be / but for someone to name you,"* he wrote. Young German poets Karoline Gunderrode, Charlotte Stieglitz and Heinrich von Kleist also kill themselves, but von Kleist, facing the beautiful landscape of Lake Wannsee, shoots and kills his girlfriend first, then describes it with a

shuddering morbidity:

Smile while the gun points / your last ideas in its gunpowder / and wait for me a minute before you leave.

Stieglitz, less selfish than Kleist, in a fit of "altruism" commits suicide to allow her husband to create literature freely:

Together we suffered / You will do better now.

Can suicide be sarcastic? Of course. The dadaist artist Jacques Vaché invited two friends to live the experience of opium, what these friends didn't know is that Vaché didn't want to die alone, thus he wrote in an ironic farewell letter, and took them with him. What was surprising, or perhaps not, was that Vaché had behaved like a coward, he was afraid of death, in the trenches of World War I, from which he had returned, stigmatized, but safe and sound, a week earlier.

Let's continue. They are followed by the British Thomas Lovell Beddoes; The Frenchman Gérard de Nerval (his real name was Gérard Labrunie), the American Vachel Lindsay, the Portuguese Antero de Quental and the Spaniards Mariano José de Larra and Angel Ganivet. The superb poet De Nerval (1808 – 1855), a brilliant

(schizophrenic) madman, hanged himself in a grate in the rue de la Vieille-Lanterne in Paris, the darkest alley he could find, according to Baudelaire. And he announced it in this almost jocular way:

Hanging with the hat on / is to deceive death in two forms / one of these days / I will woo it.

Ernest Hemigway (1899-1961), more a novelist and short story writer than a poet, but a poet after all, is an example of the organic devastation produced by alcohol and a premature old age, coupled with deep depression, which drags very easily those

that suffer it towards suicide. A suicide, which in this specific case, confirms the medical approach. But it is not always so easy to explain all the cases.

Colombians Emilio Cuervo Márquez, a Parnassian poet, Carlos Lozano and the well-known Jose Asunción Silva, who walked for several days with a bull's-eye paintes with iodine on his chest by his doctor, just in the place where he shot the deadly bullet, join the group; The Ecuadorians Cesar Dávila Andrade and Pablo Palacios; The Austrian Georg Trakl; The Bulgarian Peiu Yavórov; The Greeks Periclis Yanópulos (who, to be different, shots himself on a horse at a gallop), María Polydouri, Alexis Traianós and Kostas Kariotakis; The Portuguese Florbela Espanca and Mario de Sá Carneiro; The Swiss boxer and poet Arthur Cravan, who threw himself into the sea while visiting Mexico and disappears forever; The Argentinian Mario (Paco) López Merino; The Haitian Edmond Laforest; The French surrealists Jacques Rigaut (who founded before killing himself the "General Suicide Agency") and René Crevel; The Paraguayan Roque Vallejos Garay, psychiatrist, poet and suicide, all in one; The Uruguayan Eliseo Rafael Porta; The Bolivian Emeterio Villamil de Rada and the very young German bard Wolf von Kalckreuth (17 years old).

The great Austro-Hungarian poet Rainer Maria Rilke (1875–1926), who died of leukemia, not a suicide, tried to explain the hunger for death in poets:

"...what leads one to the afterlife? / Not looking here / slowly learned, and nothing of what happened here. Nothing. / But the pains. Especially the sorrow, / also the long experience of love: that is / everything ineffable...".

Beautiful verses but they don't end up to offer us a certainty regarding this marked predisposition.

Venezuelan poets José Antonio

Ramos Sucre, Martha Kornblith and Miyó Vestrini (born in France), Chilean Pablo de Rokha, Alfonso Echevarria Yañez and Pepita Turina, and perhaps we could include here the daughter of José Donoso, Pilar. And of course, the American modernist poet Hart Crane (1899–1932), author, among others of the celebrated book *The Bridge*, also disappears in the sea not without before, as others did and will do, announcing it to the four winds:

"In the Edge, the taste of saltpeter / calls me to be ocean / I value the distance / and I take flight".

The great Italian writer and poet Cesare Pavese (1908–1950), who supposedly commits suicide by the pain of love of the American actress Constance Dowling, expresses it with fine words: "To express in the form of art, with cathartic purpose, an interior tragedy... the only way to be saved from the abyss is to look at it and measure it and to probe and descend to it."

Perhaps poets, hypersensitive beings, feel more the silence with which the world responds when asked about its ultimate meaning (Camus). Are poets more lucid to make the tremendous decision to leave a world that has no explanation, that is absurd? But no, make no mistake, Camus is not a pessimist, let alone a suicide, on the contrary, for him suicide doesn't answer the fundamental question that life raises, but evades it. Absurdity is not an end, but a beginning, and the answer is not suicide but the hope of assuming life in a more perfect and useful way.

Are poets more lucid to make the tremendous decision to leave a world that has no explanation, that is absurd?

Maybe so, but the poets continue to kill themselves.

Hungarian Attila József, the extraordinary Russian poets Marina Tsvetaeva, Sergei Esenin and Vladimir Mayakovsky, the latter, perhaps ends his life for purely political reasons; The Franco-Basque Jon Mirande; The French Jean Pierre Duprey and Fabrice Graveraux, the Argentinians Leopoldo Lugones (also a politician and a very good essayist), Carlos Romagosa, Enrique Mendez Calzada,

María Luisa Pavlovsky, Walter Adet, Blas Castellblanch, Alfonsina Storni (well-known for her poetic work but even more by the beautiful song «Alfonsina y el mar» by Ariel Ramírez and Félix Luna, 1969), Héctor Murena kills himself with wine, like a self-destructive Bacchus, Luis Hernández and Alejandra

Pizarnik, a woman mentally unstable but a great poet who decided to die surrounded by makeup dolls.

Interesting what Leon Trotsky writes about Esenin's suicide by hanging: "Esenin was not a revolutionary. The poet was not alien to the revolution, but was not related to it; The author of *Pugachov* and *the Ballad of the Twenty-six* was an extremely intimate lyricist. But our time is not lyrical. This is why Sergei Esenin, on his own account and so early has gone away from us and his time." An "educated" way of defining suicide caused by an arbitrary and totalitarian system.

But the list is long. Romanian Paul Celan; The Catalan Gabriel Ferrater; The Uruguayans Horacio Quiroga (one of the great storytellers of the Spanish language) and Delmira Agustini; The Spaniards Alfonso Costafreda, Jose Ignacio Fuentes, who first kills his wife before cutting his neck, Vistor Ramos, José Agustín Goytisolo, Carlos Obregón, Justo Alejo, a suicidal joker who subscribes to the *Clarín magazine*, minutes before killing himself, to get it in the other world, Nicolas Arnero, Wenceslao Rodriguez, Severino Tormes, Enrico Freire, who filled the room with gas and lit a match, after writing a poem entitled *Explosion*, León Artigas, José Acillona, Alina Reyes and Pedro Casariego.

In an interesting and exhaustive investigation, also an extensive literature is reviewed, of the Spanish psychiatrists Minguez, García Alonso and Gándara *Suicide, the last verse of a poet* (2010), it is concluded that the "Exalted creativity" of poetic genius, coupled with reactive depression and high consumption of alcohol and other hard drugs explain the high number of suicides among poets. According to this and other studies, artists in general, novelists, musicians, painters, etc. have a higher prevalence of suicide than the general population, but it is the poets who take the macabre palm of self-destruction.

And they don't stop. Mexicans Jaime Torres Bodet, Carlos Díaz Dufoo, Enrique Munguía, Jorge Cuesta and Antonieta Rivas Mercado; The Norwegians Tor Jonsson and Jens Bjorneboe, that announces his suicide nothing more and nothing less than in the television; The Colombian María Mercedes Carranza; The German Inge Muller; Italians Antonia Pozzi, Primo Levi (never overcame the enormous trauma of the German concentration camps in which he was incarcerated and barely survived), Beppe Salvia and Amelia Rosselli.

The philosopher José Martín Hurtado Galves in his study on Camus tells us that "thinking is a way of living timelessly and suicide is timeless thinking", to point out with sharpness that "The suicide has hope in death because all flight is a way of appearing in the thoughts of others." It is an interesting idea because it poses the possibility of suicide as a form or desperate attempt to last in a person who usually has a very low self-esteem.

Let's continue. The Japanese Yukio Mishima, who commits harakiri; The Peruvians Armando Bazán Velázquez and José María Arguedas; The Puerto Rican Julia de Burgos, who died of pneumonia but of which there is no doubt that she killed herself by drinking; The Dominican Gastón Deligne; The Brazilians Vasco dos Reis Goncalves, Ana Cristina César and Marithelma Nostra and the North Americans Sara Teasdale, John Berryman, Sylvia Plath and Anne Sexton, who could not forgive Plath for killing herself first:

"And a little of this carbon dioxide / that well dosed makes you sleep quietly so as not to wake again / to the tedium of days".

Sad conflict to reach the death that freed Plath and Sexton, two really great poets.

Not to mention the Chilean Violeta Parra Sandoval (1917-1967),

> **[... the Exalted creativity of poetic genius, coupled with reactive depression and high consumption of alcohol and other hard drugs explain the high number of suicides among poets.**

who left us before killing herself for love —among other things— that wonderful poem that is:

Thanks to life that has given me so much / It has given me laughter and has given me tears / Thus I distinguish laughter and brokenness / The two materials that form my song / And the song of you that is the same song / And the song of all that is my own song.

Or sensitive Stefan Zweig and

the great Virginia Wolf, who left her husband a farewell: "I have lost everything except the certainty of your goodness, I cannot continue to ruin your life any longer..."

And the Cubans?

Well, Cuban poets couldn't be less, although it is worth clarifying that in several articles that we have read for the preparation of this brief essay, sometimes facts are forced, as much to include poets that weren't such, as the santiaguero Pablo Lafargue and Laura, his wife, daughter of Carlos Marx, as in attributing suicide to deaths in which one can't prove the fact, as the case, very debatable indeed, of José Martí.

Juan Cristóbal Naples Fajardo, the Cucalambé, a great poet of the nineteenth century is often cited. The truth is that we don't know of what this man died, because stricto sensu, he disappeared in 1861. Various explanations have been tried for his disappearance, including, of course, suicide, but the truth is that we don't know the cause, and since his body was never found, it is very probable that we are in the presence of one of those insoluble mysteries so attractive to speculation.

Carlos Pío Uhrbach and Juana Borrero, although they lived a history of Shakespearian love, didn't commit suicide. They could have done it, but they didn't. He died in a swamp and she died of typhoid fever in Key West, not without saying goodbye to the distant beloved:

I have dreamed in my sad nights / in my sad nights of sorrow and tears / with a kiss of impossible love / without thirst and without fire, without fever and without longing.

Esteban Borrero Echeverría (1849–1906), one of the precursors of Modernism, takes his own life. René López, the author of Barcos que pasan, commits suicide (1909) with cyanide in a Havana restaurant, just after consuming a sumptuous meal: "Tell the owner that this food will be charged in hell", he said to the embarrassed waiter, and took the poison in one gulp.

The poet Rolando Escardó dies in 1960 in a car accident (there is no evidence that it was a suicide) and Luis Rogelio Nogueras, Wichy the Red, dies because of a disease, perhaps a little strange, but explicable. The one who launched herself into the void from a building is the little-known poet Marta Vignier. And the poets Hugo Ania Mercier and Luis Marimón Tápanes also commit suicide in the city of Matanzas.

In Miami, young Eddy Campa is killed and in New York, putting an end to his fight against AIDS, Reinaldo Arenas (1943-1990), the most internationally known and most studied of all, and novelist, storyteller, polemicist and extraordinary essayist, Cuban contemporary poets. In Minnesota, shortly after leaving Cuba, Juan Francisco Pulido kills himself. In Havana, poets Raul Hernández Novás, Oscar Collazo, José Manuel Suárez Estrada (hangs himself in Lenin Park), Angel Escobar and very recently Juan Carlos Flores. Some include in these lists the official (Director of the House of the Americas) Haydee Santamaría Cuadrado, a woman who favored and protected some poets, and some not, but who can't be considered a poet herself.

Calvert Casey (1924-1969), born in Baltimore, United States, can be considered, by his own choice and for his literary

work, Cuban, commits suicide in Rome, Italy, in 1969. One such poet, like Esenin and Maiakovsky, who clashed head-on with political totalitarianism and lost the battle.

Let us close this account here, although we could add more names to the macabre list. Let us return to our initial question.

Why do poets kill themselves so often?

Well, we don't know, actually.

Yes! I just killed John Lennon!

You may say I'm a dreamer / But I'm not the only one / I hope some day you'll join us / And the world will be as one.

Hollow-point bullets, also known as expanding bullets or dum-dum projectiles, were developed from the old round musket pellets used over 200 years before, by British-colonial artillery officer Neville Bertie-Clay, at the Dum-Dum Arsenal near Calcutta, India, at the end of the XIX century.

This officer's idea was terrifyingly simple. When penetrating any soft body, whether a large hunting game or a person, the hot lead, lacking a tip, would expand and instead of going through the internal organs cleanly it would tear and shred them, multiplying the destructive effect over the tissues and exponentially increasing internal hemorrhages, producing atrocious wounds that way, which would be very hard to treat and therefore nearly always deadly.

They are not commonly used in war because the range and speed of these projectiles are way lower, being flat on front which reinforces air resistance, proving ineffective at a certain distance. Also, for the added reason that these bullets are forbidden by international treaties.

Five bullets like these are the ones that will be gifted, to be loaded on his little-used 38 special revolver manufactured by Charter Adams, a gun bought on Hawaiian armory, just next to the police station, by Atlanta sheriff's deputy Dana Reeves to a young man of unstable behavior and fixed ideas called Mark David Chapman. And officer Dana did something more besides gifting the forbidden bullets, she also taught Chapman to correctly handle his revolver with the purpose of "handling himself better" at his job as a security guard.

And like everyone else, that 25 year old Young man, Mark David Chapman, born on Forth Worth Texas on May 10th of 1955, has a history. The son of a U.S. air force sergeant, suspect of domestic abuse, and a nurse, he started consuming drugs and alcohol at age fourteen, became a Born Again Christian at seventeen, tried to kill himself with carbon monoxide under the effects of a deep depression at age twenty-three (he tells his attending psychiatrists about his visions of little people that stalk him and that he's constantly tormented by his nascent obesity) and, after a failed romance with another Born Again Christian, he married Japanese-American Gloria Hiroko Abe <His own personal Yoko Ono, who even looks like the original>, that remains her wife to this day and visits him in jail, without fail, four times a year.

In time, the Young Chapman accepted a job as a security guard, and that way he came into possession of the aforementioned 38 caliber handgun. Immediately thereafter he escapes to Honolulu for the next four weeks, living at full speed, with money borrowed by his father in law, and a short time later he travels around the world: five Asian nations, India, Lebanon, and four or five European countries with money obtained from god knows where. At age twenty-four, in September 1980, he writes to one of his many friends, Linda Irish, telling l her that he's going crazy and signing that letter as "The

Catcher in the Rye" (teenager Holden Caulfield, the main character of the eponymous book by American writer J.D. Salinger, and, a few days later, even though he tries to get rid of the bad ideas on his head for a couple of weeks, he starts lurking around the building where composer and singer John Lennon lives.

That's how we find him, on the early hours of the morning of December 8, 1980, in front of the Dakota Apartments, in New York City.

The Dakota, 1 West 72 St. Upper West Side, New York, wasn't even remotely new when Chapman stood, vigilant and obsessed, in front of the main entrance. Designed in pseudo-renaissance style by the architect of German descent Henry J. Hardenbergh, it was finished in 1884 and almost from the beginning its 65 apartments, ranging from 4 to 20 rooms, became the favorite dwelling of many among the rich and famous (and also for filmmakers, in its halls and recesses was filmed, among others, Roman Polanski's "Rosemary's Baby"), between them movie stars Boris Karloff, Lauren Bacall, José Ferrer, Jason Robards, Judy Garland and Mia Farrow; musicians, conductors, singers Ian McDonald, Bob Crewe, Roberta Flack and Leonard Bernstein; writers Aleister Crowley, Charles H. Ford and Carson McCullers; and dancer Rudolf Nureyev, among many others.

And, of course, the most famous among all: British singer John Lennon and his wife, Yoko Ono, together with their son, Sean, that

are the owners of several apartments in different floors of the building. One that they use as a living space, located on the seventh floor with seven rooms, and another for office space a floor down, and yet another to store their junk, including used and unused furniture, dozens of musical instruments, bikes that they don't use and a pair of Egyptian mummies that they purchased once and didn't even remember.

But what was Young Mark David Chapman doing that cold Monday morning of the eight of December of 1908 in the slightly anachronistic (and, for me, who has walked through it out of curiosity, quite ugly) entrance of The Dakota?

Well, young Chapman, with his small but powerful handgun loaded with the five hollow point bullets in the pocket of his coat, was getting ready to, for reasons that still aren't clear nowadays, to kill his admired, or should we say, adored, and at the same time despised, John Lennon. Lennon, who had, a few weeks before, answered a question from an interviewer of London's BBC.

"I don't fear living in New York. I've never been attacked, I've never been bothered. The only thing that happens is that, once in a while, someone stops me in the street to ask for an autograph. And for me that's not a bother, quite the contrary, it makes me feel good."

To kill, yes, you heard me, that Lennon, a bit of a drifter due to constant narcotic consumption, a little bored in his golden cage and under the not inquisitive but rather inquisitorial watch of Ono, a sort of pocket-size Asian tiger, he wakes up at four in the morning without the help of an alarm clock to watch the sunrise over Central Park. That how it's told by Charlie Swan, also known as The Oracle, or O, the man that read the Tarot cards daily to Yoko Ono, especially to guide her in business. And also, useful to entertain John, who has his own cards read every day and is a little worried because the card of "Death" is coming up repeatedly. But he calms down when Swan reassures him that the card also means "rebirth" and that 1981, next year, will be one of great importance and definitive in his extraordinary life.

Thank goodness, Lennon must have thought, with a sigh of relief. But if Lennon was troubled, who wasn't? Even if we leave aside the aforementioned Death card.

Let's not forget, looking from a distance we think it's something ludicrous, that John Lennon, who wasn't an American citizen, had serious discrepancies with the FBI, and generally with the entire American establishment, that were his declared enemies, just as he was theirs, at least according to his lip service. Lennon despaired about his residency status, that "fucking status" that forced to spend time, and that really drove him mad, in lawyers and paperwork. And he had family issues, and with his old friend, and even with Yoko Ono herself, that after giving birth to Sean flatly refused – this was an often-repeated piece of gossip – to have sex with him and it was rumored among insiders, that she had a lover. Petty details, but if it stings it must be for a reason. Oh! He composed every now and then, like when he sat down on his piano (he used to do this during marathon streaks of work to later return to his contemplative life and his narcotic numbness) and pulled that wonder that is "Imagine" out of his head.

Chapman is still lurking around the entrance of The Dakota and ends up, not surprisingly, talking with Lennon, and from him he obtains and autograph scrawled over the cover of the album "Double Fantasy", a recently released record of which Lennon didn't feel very proud of, even though it became an instant hit.

But Lennon did more than that. He looked Chapman in the face through his nearsighted glassed and asked him with a benevolent gesture, quite typical of him when he was in a good mood – Is that all you want? – And waited for an answer. Chapman, perplexed, nodded and mumbled incoherently. And Paul Goresh, John's occasional friend, and amateur photographer that was passing by left a graphic record of the moment.

A photographic image of very poor artistic quality taken from a cheap camera, one of those unexpected strokes of luck that later take

on great historical interest. After Lennon walks away down the street, the flabbergasted Chapman, away tells Goresh "They're never going to believe this in Hawaii!" Goresh nods and continues his course. Lennon keeps on walking calmly towards his White automobile, he used to par kit on the street for convenience although he could've parked it in the big garages of The Dakota, and he goes to work for a while to Record Plant, a studio near Broadway and the 44th.

What is John doing on Record Plant? Well, editing and putting the backing guitars to a Yoko Ono record, for which the fucking Jap has stubbornly determined to be the singer. And he doesn't want to, or can't say no, because that's how men that desperately need a mother are.

The afternoon and early evening both go by peacefully, although Chapman, Lennon doesn't know, never stops lurking around the place. He speaks with the regular crowd, with the security guards, invoked his fanaticism for the Beatles and for Lennon, annoys, tires, but he learns and knows everything about the schedules and habits of the Lennon-Ono family.

Around half past ten at night John comes back from the recording studio with Yoko Ono, they're hungry, but decide to eat something in the apartment to say goodbye to Sean and go to bed. They park the car on 72nd. street, as usual, and walk to the entrance of The Dakota. Ono, also as usual, walks fast and goes in front. Chapman comes out of the shadows under the archway and greets her, but Yoko, something very usual in her, given her surly and arrogant nature, doesn't pay attention to him and cuts him off; without even looking at him, as if he didn't exist.

A taxi driver that was making a stop in front of the building and the doorman, José Sanjenís Perdomo, with whom Chapman has spoken several times, where watching the young man coming and going <with his bag slung on his shoulder, in which he carried his worn out copy of The Catcher in the Rye, that according to him he had read fifteen times and a newer, unopened copy, plus a Bible to which he had added to the "Gospel according to John… Lennon"> by the 72nd. Street and surrounding areas all afternoon and later stop under the shadow of the archway of The Dakota.

Then Chapman, apparently at ease, lets Yoko Ono go without insisting and when Lennon is almost next to him, calls him by his name "Hey, John, hey". He stops hesitating and looks at the young man to whom he had signed the record that morning, but doesn't seem to recognize him, perhaps because it's a little dark, or because there are just too many people that ask for his autograph. Chapman then, in a quick move and without adding a word, gets in fighting position, knee to the floor, and shoots the five dum dum bullets in quick succession, four of which hit the target and another, grazing Johns head, hits a door frame and gets flattened there.

The four remaining projectiles penetrate Lennon's left side (it's been widely speculated that Chapman was at his right, but that might be explained with the turn made by John when called by his name, or maybe not, god only knows), three come out and one remains lodged in the victim's body. Four entry wounds, three exit wounds. A true massacre.

John Lennon says, "I've been shot!", Walks a few steps to the security booth, stumbles up three steps and falls to the ground. One of the building's security guards, comes running, takes Chapman's gun from his hand, tosses it away and screams "Look at what you've done!" and a profanity. Chapman replies with trembling voice "Yes, I just killed John Lennon!" Another version says "I just shot" instead of killed, and yet another denied that there was such exchange. The truth is that Yoko Ono, that was already near the elevators, runs back and starts screaming asking for someone to call the police, or an ambulance, or whoever, but to call someone.

Chapman, indifferent, with strange calmness, puts his backpack on the floor, sticks his face to the wall and waits for the police with raised arms. Agent Steven Spiro, who's two blocks away in a patrol car nearby arrives at the scene, asks what happened, is pointed towards the killer and arrests Chapman, grabbing him by the neck. He turns him around and cuffs him with his hands behind his backs. It isn't known whether or not he reads him his Miranda rights, but Chapman doesn't care. What matters is that he doesn't lose his backpack.

Yoko Ono tries to talk to Lennon, but after mumbling something like "Now! It had to be now!" Or "Not now!", he loses consciousness. Ono picks John's bloodied Windsor glasses from the ground and puts them in a pocket of her coat.

Policeman John Moran, who comes running behind, realizes that Lennon is losing too much blood and decides not to wait for the ambulance. He picks him up from the floor trying to make him stand, but Lennon collapses. He asks him if he's really John Lennon, but doesn't get any answer. He realizes that he's wasting his time, literally carries him and takes him in his squad car, with the siren and all the lights on, to St. Luke's-Roosevelt Hospital Center. Meanwhile, patrol cars keep arriving at the 82nd. Street precinct, just a few blocks away.

One of them insults Chapman, but the others calm him down. While some start to cordon off the crime scene, others take away the killer, handcuffed and held strongly by both arms, to the station in a squad car. Sergeant Anthony Palma takes care of Yoko Ono and also takes her to the hospital in his car.

Meanwhile, Doctor Stephan Lynn and his team take care of the wounded. They try to get fluids into his body through his veins, but these cannot be found. They've all collapsed due to the acute hipovolemia brought about by the terrible hemorrhage. They administer air with a mask and notice it escapes through the wounds on his back, unequivocally proving that both lungs are damaged. They perform a thoracotomy without anesthetics; but actually John has been dead for a while, and they observe, very professionally, the internal damage caused by the hollow-point bullets

They can't even give him manual heart massage because his heart has been ruptured in several places. The thoracic aorta is open from top to bottom, and both lungs are pierced in both back and front. John has lost around 90% of his circulating blood and his vital organs, heart, lungs and aorta are torn apart. He's pronounced dead. The whole process has lasted around twenty minutes. Pathologist Elliot M. Gross, who will sign the autopsy, will later say that no human being could've lived more than a minute or two with such internal injuries.

The picture of John Lennon in the morgue, the only one in existence, was slyly taken by a morgue employee who sold it for ten thousand dollars. Copies of the death certificate magically appeared and were sold, and are still sold today, at different prices, some of them truly outrageous. Even Yoko Ono kept John's blood-stained glasses without cleaning them and used them on the cover of an album years later.

John Lennon was cremated and there was no funeral.

Here's where the facts, the tangible reality, ends, and the legends starts. The why and how can be discussed about ad infinitum. And this is also where the conspiracy theories start, that started to pop up like mushrooms almost as soon as sportscaster Howard Cossell stopped transmission during a football game between the Miami Dolphins and the New England Patriots to be the first one to break the news, a huge journalistic scoop.

But those assumptions, distortions of reality, unexplainable attitudes, and conspiracy theories aren't the main reason for this article, so… Oops! I found out, during my research, that a person whose name has remained anonymous delivered the record that Chapman gave to John Lennon to sign. This person gave it away to the police some time later (it was supposedly found discarded in a garden near The Dakota, and, not being considered an important piece of evidence, it was returned to the carrier. The record was sold years later for half a million dollars.

That's not a legend. That was a great piece of business.

But the truth is that John Lennon was gone, never to return.

The strange death of Julián del Casal

What illness or accident led Julián del Casal to such an early death? Was it really a fit of laughter and the subsequent rupture of an aneurysm, as it has been told over and over again?

To yearn for death, your own death, and to announce it to the whole world, even though it has no fixed date, is not considered normal today —nor tasteful— in a socially and psychologically healthy person.

But if we travel to the last decade of the nineteenth century, it doesn't matter if our starting point is a literary hall in Mexico City, a poor and «spiritually sensitive» loft in Paris or a traditional family home in Havana, and the people you know are recognized poets, true poets, regardless of whether they are romantics, modernists or symbolists, the subject adopts other more complicated nuances.

Let us take a particular case where it is openly stated that persistent and macabre desire to put an end to life.

Arrebatadme al punto de la tierra,
que estoy enfermo y solo y fatigado
y deseo volar hacia la altura,
porque allí debe estar lo que yo he amado.

In fact, it is a quatrain of a poem *Black and White* of the Cuban Julián del Casal y de la Lastra (1863-1893), one of those poets, true poets, who saw, or claimed to see, the Lady of the Scythe as a close and timely friend who was waiting with hope and without fear while writing, as in a kind of waiting time, good poetry.

Let's look at this other segment of the poem *La agonía de Petronio*, in which Julián del Casal supposedly refers to the final moments of the elegant and dissolute Roman senator Gaius Petronius Arbiter (27–66 A.D.), sentenced to death by Emperor Nero, but in which you feel the Cuban bard's longing to finish his not so stimulating life, his economic conditions were bad, his housing was poor, the social denial he faced due to his homosexuality and the colony of the island were asphyxiating, in a high end and worthy of being remembered and even emulated by the (very few) related souls around him.

Y como se doblega el mustio nardo,
dobló su cuello el moribundo bardo,
libre por siempre de mortales penas
aspirando en su lánguida postura
del agua perfumada la frescura,
y el olor de la sangre de sus venas.

In short, a man, a great poet of his time, longing for and idealizing the transit of earthly life to that other, for him sublime, from which no one has returned.

And in fact, the inexorable Death pleased him and rewarded him with a premature death, as early as twenty-nine years of age (he was a month away to turn thirty), which didn't prevent, and it's a valid observation, an important literary work worthy of appearing, side by side, alongside that of the precursors and creators of the important literary movement called modernism: the Cuban (although he lived almost all his active life outside the island) José Martí, the Colombian José Asunción Silva, Mexicans Manuel Gutiérrez Nájera, Salvador Díaz Mirón and Amado Nervo, Peruvian Jose Santos Chocano, Uruguayan Delmira Agustini, Spanish Salvador Rueda (the list of Spanish poets related in one way or another to modernism is long and includes, among many others, the two Machado brothers) and, of course, the greatest of all, as a modernist poet, the Nicaraguan Félix Rubén García Sarmiento, known worldwide as Rubén Darío.

Precisely the latter, Rubén Darío, with whom Julian had written from 1887 and whom he met personally in Havana in 1892, had much to do with the posthumous recognition of the Cuban, not forgetting Rueda, perhaps the most relevant Spanish modernist poet, who in Madrid also received him with enthusiasm, although fleetingly, in the only trip abroad that the Cuban could make in his brief life. A trip, by the way, frustrated, because his goal was Paris and he didn't had enough money to get there.

The truth is that many of these bards would die young. José Martí fell fighting, an absurd death that bordered suicide, to the Spanish troops, during the denominated War of Cuban Independence, at 42 years of age; José Asunción Silva takes his life at 31; Manuel Gutiérrez Nájera is killed by hemophilia at 35 and Delmira Agustini is murdered by her husband at age 27. If we were to pick a little among the second-line modernists the list would increase much more.

But, returning to our character... what illness or accident led Julián del Casal to such an early death? Was it really a fit of laughter and the subsequent rupture of an aneurysm, as has been told over and over and as it is outlined in all its brief and rather repetitive biographies and, of course, Wikipedia?

Well, the author of this essay has serious doubts about it. Let's review what has been said about this, which is not much.

Two sources of information prevail. The first is Julián himself, who in several personal letters refers to his illnesses as "a dark evil, unknown by doctors, without cure" (Julián del Casal's letter to Rubén Darío), and in another letter, "attacked with cruel pains, I don't know if rheumatic or nervous... well, all the symptoms of a great anemia that threatens to devour me."

Julián's comments about his deteriorated health were many and varied, he also spoke of bumps partial paralyzes of arms and legs, loss of vision and other symptoms, and expressed both through his correspondence and private conversations as in his own poetic work, as we have seen in the initial quatrain with which we began this brief essay.

The other source, less explicit, was his doctor, Dr. Francisco Zayas. A Cuban doctor from which we can say little, as the Cuban writer Antón Arrufat says in an excellent work (to which I owe much) about him: "we know little of Doctor Zayas as a doctor, except that he had literary inclinations." Well, this doctor had diagnosed del Casal with "tumors in the lungs" and then "the rupture of an aneurism" (without specifying where) as the last cause of the sudden and tumultuous death of the poet.

Truth is, and our only really objective reference, is that del Casal was dining at the house of Dr. Lucas de los Santos Lamadrid, located on Paseo del Prado in the city of Havana (still preserved, although in a dilapidated state), when laughing out loud, those who knew him agree that the poet, languid and depressive, was not given to these effusions, of an occurrence of one of the guests, suffered a kind of spasm and began to vomit blood, red, in abundant quantities. The poet died shortly thereafter, probably due to asphyxiation, airway obstruction by accumulated blood, we believe.

There is no record or reference whatsoever that an autopsy was performed on the corpse of Julián del Casal.

This is what we have been able to ascertain so far, from the medical point of view, about the obvious chronic illness of Julián del Casal, his abrupt and apparently unexpected death when he was "improving his ills" as Arrufat refers to in the aforementioned article.

What, then, is our professional opinion about the illness and death of this patient of only 29 years of age?

The first thing is to ask how one could diagnose "lung tumors" in a patient who obviously, this weren't available to physicians at the time, had no radiological or endoscopic studies of any kind. The logical thing is to think that del Casal suffered from chronic pulmonary tuberculosis, a condition that was undermining his health in a progressive way and was also very common at that time. Pulmonary tuberculosis, except for rest and more or less good nutrition, had no treatment at that time.

The "strange death" from a supposed aneurysm (it would have to have been an arterial aneurysm piercing the upper gastrointestinal tract or upper respiratory tract, which is highly unlikely and less so in a person of that age) seems to us simply a diagnostic mistake (or it was preferred, for social reasons and friendship, not to speak of the true cause), obviating the much more common massive hemoptysis coming from a tuberculous cave.

I remember my old teachers, —I'm talking about forty years ago— who told me about the heroic age, today almost forgotten, of the antituberculous sanatoriums (La Esperanza or Topes de Collantes, for example) and how those patients, most of them chronic, died in a few minutes because of hemoptysis that today seem almost impossible. Hemoptysis for which there was no effective treatment until the onset of the very mutilating thoracic surgeries —costal repairs and compressions of the affected part of the lung— that brought the twentieth century in its first two decades and which were still practiced until the fifties.

Today, with potent antibiotic treatments for tuberculosis, these sudden deaths and extraordinary drama seem almost impossible, but at that time they were the norm.

The rest of the symptoms reported by del Casal are attributed to the evolutionary deterioration caused by untreated pulmonary tuberculosis, perhaps to some joint component of the same disease (common, again, at that time), to the immunological degradation of the condition and Hypochondria and chronic depression —how not be depressed with so many problems and disenchantments?— of the patient.

Of course all this is an academic exercise in the void, but it seems reasonable and interesting to ask from time to time for some of the "certainties" repeated by our history, both literary and the political, official.

Maybe we are left to just wonder what could have been and wasn't.

What poetic and literary peaks would Julián del Casal have achieved if he had lived a normal life, or had been told in those days with an effective treatment for his illness?

No one can answer that question.

We are surprised, of course, with how much he achieved while suffering from such bad health and in such a short time.

Did Oscar Wilde die of sorrow?

Early in the morning on October 10, 1900 —closed year that for some was the start of the 20th. century, so far the bloodiest and most deranged of the relatively few centures that humanity has lived—, otorhinolaringology professor Maurice A'Court Tucker, assited by physician Paul Cleiss, performed surgery on a room in the d'Alsace Hotel in Paris (that wasn't infrequent back then among people of certain economi status and hotels were probably safer than the dismal hospitals of the time), to patient Oscar Fingal O'Flahertie Wills Wilde, born 46 years before in Dublin, Ireland.

The surgery performed on the noted patient was, almost surely, a radical mastoidectomy under chloroform anaesthetic. A very bloody technique —the mastoid bone was perforated by a hand drill until reaching the middle and internal ear— execured to drain a purulent abscess, consequence of a chrinic otitis acquire by the patient due to an unclear injury, suffered while in prison four years before.

The post-surgical progression of the patient was relatively good for the first few weeks, but afterwards he presented pain in the affected ear, in the etes, in the face and all over his head, that increased at times, very high fever in bursts, shakiness, sweating, and a series of neurological disorders that indicated a recurrence of the ear infection, complicated now by an acute bacterial meningoencephalitis. Not to mention that in the pre-antibiotic age there wasn't even a remotely adecuate treatment for a a complication of such magnitude. All they could do, if anything, was praying.

The patient passed away, already unconscious, on November 30th. of the same year 1900, less than two months after the surgical procedure. Life had been good to the deceased, known around the world as Oscar Wilde, until around six years before, in which love, that bastard, dragged him into disgrace.

Let's review, very briefly, the biography of Oscar Wilde.

His father, William Wilde, was famous and wealthy —an otorhinolatingologist, by an ironic twist of fate— and his mother, Jane, was a known artist and political activist (she used to write virulently Irish nationalist poetry under the pseudonym «Speranza» but everyone knew it was her). In his childhood, thanks to nursemaids and governesses he learned French and German with correctitude and during his adolescence and youth he studied the Greek and Latin classics scrupulously, which gave him an ample and solid cultural background and a refined and precise use of language. He had a youthful affair with the beautiful Florence Balcombe that ended abruptly when she abandoned Oscar for Bram Stoker, author of *Dracula*.

The failed romance with Balcome seems to have been very painful to him. From that experience he left us the phrase: *"two sweet years, the sweetest years of all my youth"* that Oscar wrote in reference to the two years of romance with the girl, in a hurtful but very corteous and restrained letter, and perhaps there was also a profound and quite misgiving about his own masculinity, but I'm just especulating.

A few years later, having definitely settled in London, he met the exquisite and naïve Constance Lloyd, whom he married and had two children with; Cyril, the firstborn, and Vyvyan, just a year later. It's been discussed a lot among Wilde's biographers about Constance's second pregnancy — it seems that she gained a lot of weight, which caused stretchmarks, and also spots on her face and legs— which made caused Oscar, although sadly, to reject her sexually. We don't know what was going on in his head, but we know that homosexuality was a punishable crime in Victorian England, and even for a long while afterwards (the suicide of the prosecuted and condemned mathematical genius and war hero Alan Turing after World War Two evidences it), which led a lot of people into unwanted marriages, even some of them arranged, and most of the time unhappy.

But this storm was occuring only in Wilde's personal world. For the outside world, Wilde's marriage was one devoid of financial hardships, well conducted and happy, and Oscar's fame as an author an playwright was, with his wife's support, growing after the publication of The Picture of Dorian Grey, The Importance of Being Earnest, Lady Windermere's Fan, The Happy Prince and Other Stories, A Woman of No Importance, An Ideal Husband and other hits that have lasted to this day. We may point out that the victorian residence in which Constance, Oscar, and their children lived is still today a very popular touristic destination.

Hence, everything was going well, very well, until... until Oscar met Bosie, known among the British aristocracy as Lord Alfred Douglas, a youn aristocrat and cherished son of the Marquis of Queensberry. Oscar lost his mind for the boy (life would prove he wasn't that much of one) and started making mistakes. The most

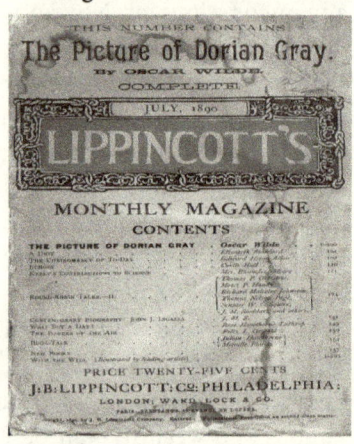

severe of them all was to let himself be manipulated by Bosie into accusing the Marquis of defamation —libel, actually— based on a personal letter that the man had given Wilde as an insult (Queensberry was convince that Oscar had pulled his «angelic» son towards the wrong track) and in which he had written: For Oscar Wilde posing Somdomite, just like that, with capital S and an m in the middle.

Take into account that, had the crime of «libel» been proven, the Marquis could've even been sent to jail. But even though Lord Marquis could write certain offensive things under the influence of rage, he wasn't a fool in regards or tribunals and advocates, and the one that had already thrown himself in the midst of lawyers and courts was Oscar, enticed by the devious Bosie.

To get rid of the accusation of «libel», the Marquis only had to prove that what he had wtitten in the aforementioned letter was true (the crime of libel could only exist if it was a proven slander) and if he proved it, which didn't seem too difficult given Oscar's unbridled affection for Bosie (and for others before, like young Robert Ross), well, then the one that would have to go to jail was Oscar, for sodomy.

On top of that, Oscar, who deep down was a cantanke-

rous, didn't try to defend himself conservatively by trying to prove his innocence, but rather tried to appeal to a theory that he had devised and which he termed «amorality of art». In other words, his relationship with Bosie was a form of "art" and art isn't moral or inmoral, but amoral. Needless to say, this sunk him further, making him a subject of outrage and mockery among the members of London's high society, a group of which he had been part until very recently.

He was condemned to two years in prison. In that relatively brief period (for poor Oscar that time felt endless) he met the prisons of Newgate, Pentonville, Wandworth, and Reading Gaol, the latter the worst of the all, which doesn't mean that the others were any good. None of the sort, and think, dear reader, what that signified at the time—and previos times, and later times—going to prison for sodomy.

In Reading he was placed on the cell number three of the third floor of ward C (third letter of the alphabet) = 333 and, maybe out of pity or thanks to the respect that his social status and fame gave him, he was allowed some books and some paper that he spent almost completely writing lenghty letters to Bosie, letters that he later denied ever getting.

Bosie, and no one will be surprised by this, abandoned him for other men. His wife, Constance, also left him, changed her name and legally removed any custody rights he might have over his two children. He, almost immediately after getting out of prison, having turned into a shadow of his former self, sailed towards the continent and never again got back to British or Irish soil. This is the period his biographers have denominated as Oscar Wilde's French exile.

He tried —he was still quite young and might have had a scrap of faith on himslef and others— to join a congregation in the «Society of Jesus», an institution in the Catholic Church that welcomed repentful sinners, but he was rejected. Sodomy was too much for them. He ended up then, what else, on the arms of his former lover Robert Ross, who had a villa in the coast of the north of France. Oscar, without a doubt, could've yelled «I called onto the heavens but they weren't listening».

There he wrote *The ballad of Reading Gaol*, which isn't about his hardships in jail, how many that have read it choose to believe, but about the execution of convict Charles Thomas Wooldridge, and then… well, he reunited with Bosie in Rouen. That meeting wasn't long, since Bosie's family threatened to cut him off, and Constance, used to send something to Oscar in secret every now and then, also warned him that she wouldn't do it again if he pursued that relationship.

> «Sometimes we can spend years without living at all, and suddenly all of our life is concentrated in a single instant».

That was the end.

In one of his essays Wilde had written: «Sometimes we can spend years without living at all, and suddenly all of our life is concentrated in a single instant».

Clinically, Oscar Wilde died from complications of an ear infection, but... Isn't it possible that he died of sorrow?

From what did the Little Girl of Guatemala actually die?

Let's start with a description and anecdote that I think are interesting.

In August of 2013, in a roundabout of Avenida de las Americas, an important roadway that crosses the entire center of Guatemala City, capital of the nation of the same name, was inaugurated a statue of the Cuban José Martí, a garden square also called José Martí and a strip with a few verses engraved in bronze of the poet and politician dedicated to María García Granados y Saborío (1860-1878), the young woman we all know as "La Niña de Guatemala".

The monument, as a whole, is modern, large and above all

Can death by love be scientifically proven?

very attractive for the walker because of the trees and plants that surround it and the sense of calm that they transmit. The total height of the statue, counting the sturdy base —which was built for a different purpose since 1973— and the complete body figure of the hero is nine meters and the design and sculptural work was done by the Cuban artists Andrés González and Oscar Luis González, who, curiously, executed it with a new —for sculptural art— ferrocement assembly technique.

The opening ceremony was attended by the Foreign Minister of the Republic of Guatemala, the Cuban ambassador, other officials, politicians, journalists and about two hundred others, including Cubans who have long lived in Guatemala. But for me the anecdote is that the mayor of the capital, who is serving his sixth term in that position, the most important businessman and former president of the republic Alvaro Arzú Irigoyen (who also has a television program in which travels and describes places of historical and touristic interests of the city that he governs and which recalls the well-known *Andar La Habana* with Eusebio Leal), at the end of his brief speech, he turned to the Unesco ambassador in the country, born in Cuba, and said: —Well, sir, Martí made it difficult for María and we make him a statue, as you can see, we have no grudges! The anecdote was told to me personally by him, as we walked through the garden square José Martí, the recipient of Arzú's words, Ambassador Carranza.

As Cubans, accustomed, and taught, always to see in

José Martí, as he would say, only the light, never the stains, the assertion of Alvaro Arzú takes us somewhat unaware. Could a man who was once called "Saint of America, Apostle, Teacher, Eponymous Hero, National Hero" and dozens of other adjectives, all sublime and dithyrambic, do something ugly to someone? And not to anybody or any political opponent but to a very young person, spiritually healthy and above all who was willing to die of love for him and eventually did. For Alvaro Arzú and probably for many Guatemalans, obviously the answer is yes.

But... is it that, perhaps, dying from love, that romantic, nebulous and somewhat contradictory action in which the woman in love dies for the beloved man who really or supposedly despises her, or vice versa, is something unheard of in the history of humanity. No way. Cemeteries all over the world, red chronicles, hospital corps, psychiatric consultations, history, and especially the history of art and literature are full of cases and examples. Let us briefly review a few of these examples, ancient and modern, which remain in our cultural reservoir:

• Dido, the first and mythical queen of the African Carthage, as Virgil tells us in the Aeneid, commits suicide for Aeneas' love, the hero who tries to reach the Italian peninsula at all costs —it's his inexcusable destiny— and therefore leaves the woman in love who can't, and shouldn't, follow him. Although Aeneas loves Dido, he interposes in that love the fateful fate of the gods, duty. Thus Virgil tells us: "But among all the unhappy Fenisa, already doomed to her fatal destiny, doesn't satisfy herself by looking, and the more she lights up the more she looks, and her excitement increases, as well as the gifts and the beautiful child."

• The beautiful and free nymph Echo, according to mythology, despised all men, but as almost always happens, one day (a bad day) she met Narcissus in the forest, and fell hopelessly in love. The problem is that Echo had already been cursed, precisely for her beauty, for the more than jealous and vengeful goddess Hera with the loss of voice, worse, with the obligation to repeat the last word heard by her interlocutor and only that. Narcissus, a simple soul, laughed at this defect of poor Echo, and she, shattered, committed suicide by locking herself in a cave and ceasing to eat and drink until she died of hunger and thirst. Narcissus paid his mockery a little later, but that's another story.

• Samson, passionately in love with the Philistine Delilah, and vilely betrayed by her, ends, after many and very varied vicissitudes, killing himself and killing all his enemies under the weight of the roof of the temple demolished by his enormous strength. For more details read the Book of Judges of the Old Testament and all that has been written after (and painted and sung and musicalized) about the mythical fact. A tragedy unleashed by... what else, by love.

- Lefkada was called the mythical cliff from which the unrequited lovers of the island of Lesbos threw themselves into the sea to die. And of course, the most famous one who died from love from that rock was Sappho of Mytilene (c600 ANE). She wrote before committing suicide (supposedly) this sad farewell: "I really want to die, I want to, because that one crying left me. And when she left, she said to me, O Sappho, what a terrible pain ours is, that, without my desire, I leave you."

- Cleopatra (c69-30 ANE), queen of Egypt, commits suicide (with the asp in the basket and all that we already know) before the irreparable loss of her husband — who wasn't the first— Marco Antonio and his kingdom. Did Cleopatra love Marco Antonio so much as to kill herself for him or did the good lady only want his political power, now lost? I don't know, nor do I think I'll ever know, but I sense that things of power and politics tend to be much stronger than those of the heart.

- Geneva, queen of Camelot and adored wife of King Arthur (around the 6th century NE) actually loves in silence the knight Sir Lancelot. It is an impossible and tragic love that ends with the destruction of the Round Table and the death of the good King Arthur and all the Knights of the Grail. Truly a disaster, however the two, Geneva and Lancelot, died of age, loving each other in the distance and supposedly without ever having erotic contact. I think this is not an appropriate example because those who die of (because of) love are the others. A proof of the devastating, unjust and sometimes lethal force of passionate love.

- The case of the young Francesca of Rimini is much more tragic because her passion for Paolo, her husband's brother, led the latter (a case of extreme domestic violence) to kill them both. The story, based on a real event (around 1284 NE), is told to us by Dante in the *Divine Comedy* but after him there are written poems, plays, operas, symphonies and even the sculpture *The Kiss*, from Auguste Rodin , inspired by this misfortune. *Here the death from love*, as seen, was imposed by another's hand.

- The Mexican princess Iztaccihuatl, mistakenly confused by

her father who wanted to marry her with another military man of higher rank, died from love for the warrior Popocatepetl, whom she believed was dead. The warrior then, knowing his loved one was dead, died from love for the princess in an act of magnificent reciprocity. Both, turned into great volcanoes, look at us today — and perhaps threaten us— from the horizon (unfortunately tarnished by smog) when we visit the Mexican Valley.

• From love died the lovers of Teruel, Isabel de Segura and Juan Marinez de Marcilla (around the thirteenth century). The story has been told and recreated time and again by Tirso de Molina, the musician Tomás Bretón y Hernandez, the writer Mariano Miguel de Val and many others. If you ever visit Teruel, in Spain, don't miss going to the old Church of San Pedro. There is the beautiful mausoleum of the two lovers, side by side, who almost, almost, take each other's hands. Believe me, it's worth seeing.

• The deaths from love of Callisto and Melibea (Callisto actually dies from a home accident) are indeed tragic. La Celestina is the title of the work, written at the end of the fifteenth century, which is usually attributed to the graduate Fernando de Rojas. The subtitle of the so-called tragicomedy says in part: "... composed in rebuke of the madmen in love who, overcome by their disordered appetite...". A good and very sensible warning.

• What about Romeo and Juliet? William Shakespeare, with his immortal work (published for the first time c1597) makes literary and popular paradigmatic the deaths from love. There is beauty, doubtless, in those last verses that Juliet declares just before killing herself: "Yea, noise? then I'll be brief. O happy dagger! This is thy sheath; there rust, and let me die."

• Suicide from love of the young Werther (Goethe, 1774) marked an era and made the German poet an early literary star. Is Werther killed by the unrequited love of his beloved, married to another, Lotte or simply by love of romantic love? In fact all the same. Werther dies of love. That's it.

• Karoline von Gunderrode (1780-1806), poet and romantic writer herself, pierced her heart with a silver stiletto and dropped it down the Rhine River (no doubt she wanted to die). Did she do so out of frustrated love with the writer Georg Creuzer or because of the popular trend, then in all its heyday, of Werther?

Whatever it is, she died of love, didn't she?

- Anna Karenina, Leon Tolstoy's character (published in 1877) commits suicide for love in an atrocious way —she throws herself under the wheels of a train— but we are left with the question of whether it is because of the love that moves away more and more from her of the dissolute Vronsky or by the "love" to her lost previous life and the consequent humiliation. You decide because Master Tolstoy wisely leaves us in uncertainty.

- Leonor Izquierdo (1894-1912) was the woman (actually the girl) and inspiring muse of the Spanish poet Antonio Machado. She didn't die of cold, but of tuberculosis, but she could perfectly well have died of love for the bard, a love that she demonstrated at all times and in an absolute way. Machado wrote about the peaceful resting-place of the lost lover: "With the first lilies and the first roses of the orchards, on a blue afternoon she climbs the Espino, the high Espino where her land is."

- Mariano José de Larra (1809-1837), the great Spanish journalist, columnist and politician, shot himself in the head by the love of Dolores Armijo, his demanding and fickle lover until that tragic moment. No doubt he loved her enough to give up a very promising career and die for her.

- Amedeo Modigliani (1884-1920) was a painting genius, and was also a disaster as a person: party animal, alcoholic, drug addict, female abuser, disordered almost to the edge of sociopathy, in short, a bad boy, but was, as it usually happens to these gentlemen, extraordinarily lucky in love. Women killed themselves, metaphorically and even literally for him. A test. Jeanne Hébuterne (1898-1920), the mother of his daughter, who is eight and a half months pregnant for the second time, sits back on the window of her parents' house, a fifth floor, the day after the painter's funeral and dropped herself. She commits suicide and kills the child she carried inside so she will not live without Modigliani. Passion, immaturity (she was 21 years old), madness, extreme irresponsibility? Who knows.

- British actress Lucy Gordon (1980-2009), with a promising career ahead, probably hung herself for the love of a man who had committed suicide, perhaps for another woman, months before. Does anyone doubt that life is, besides tragic, often incomprehensible?

- The loves of the Chilean singer-songwriter Violeta Parra (1917-1967) were several and extraordinarily passionate, although little reciprocated. She was depressed and alone, and gave herself a bullet in the head at forty-nine years of age. She left us the song, perhaps the most contradictory in the history of music: "Thanks to life that has given me so much, it has given me laughter and has given me tears, thus I distinguish happiness and brokenness, the two materials that form my song, and the song of you that is the same song, and the song of all that is my own song". Have fear, dear reader, to the excess of love to life, or better, have fear to all the excesses.
- One more example, indeed debatable, to end this random list. Was the guerrilla and Cuban revolutionary leader Haydée Santamaría (1923-1980) killed for love? Is love worth, not to another being, but to a utopia that is undone, in this case the so-called Cuban Revolution, as a cause to kill oneself? I think so, at least in this specific case.

Books could be (and have been) written on the subject of death for love, a theme that is already very clearly defined in the 15th century Provencal poetry, the golden age of the so-called Courtly Love, a way of loving (and of living and suffering) that Jorge Manrique (1440-1479) very well defines with his verses: "Love is so strong a force that it forces all reason; A force of such a sort, that every brain converts, in its force and its liking; A forced striving, which can not be overcome, whose strongest force, we make more powerful, by wanting to defend it."

In fact, an anthology of prose, poems and lyrics of arias and songs that speak of dying for love or dying of love would be monumental. But as we wait for those volumes, let us return to María.

From what did the Little Girl of Guatemala actually die of?

Well, according to José Martí, the most direct and probably most involved in the affair, she died of love.

And can death by love be scientifically proven?

If we strictly adhere to this psychological phenomenon (or psychobiological because there are proven disorders in the production of certain neurotransmitters during the peak period of the event) called "love" as a single etiological cause for death, the truth is that it can't be proved, at least at the current level of medical knowledge. But if we accept intermediate causes such as deep reactive depression leading to extreme physical deterioration, abandonment of treatment of certain prior illnesses or to suicide, then yes.

As a medical curiosity (we have never personally seen a case in the course of our already long clinical practice) we note that Japanese cardiologists have recently described a syndrome they call *Takotsubo's Cardiomyopathy* or *Broken Heart Syndrome*, an acute and aberrant failure of contractility of the cardiac muscle —the myocardium doesn't rupture in the strict sense but it deforms— produced by an overload or accute stress. In these cases —exceptionally rare— death, due to acute heart failure, occurs very rapidly and is always surrounded by very dramatic signs and symptoms, which is not the case in those languid deaths and prolonged outcomes that supposedly unrequited love causes.

But let's go back to La Niña de Guatemala. Martí gives us more clues: "They entered the river late, the doctor took her out, dead. They say she died of cold; I know she died of love." If we stick literally to these verses Martí is confirming the suicide of María García Granados, either by drowning (thus the English writer Virginia Woolf and the Swiss-Argentine poet Alfonsina Storni died) or a very common pneumonic complication in the pre-antibiotic era in a presumably tubercular person.

And we say presumably tuberculous because there are versions, especially from María's relatives and friends and acquaintances and the family who refer to a chronic lung disease, a respiratory condition that María had to take care of. Pulmonary tuberculosis, as we all know, was a very frequent disease in young people in those days.

In an interesting article by Mayra Beatriz Martínez, it is even mentioned, based on indirect sources, the possibility that Martí had visited María García Granados in her terminal patient's bed and shortly before her death, a fact that would distort the dramatic turn of the famous IX poem of the Versos Sencillos. If that assumption were true, even though the episode in the river —or lake, so common in Guatemala— might have been true as an intercurrent factor, the death of the patient would almost certainly be related to an acute chronic lung disease.

Let us then try a differential diagnosis. In María García Granados her death can be attributed to:

1- A suicide by immersion (if we are guided by the verses of Martí).

2- The acceleration of a pulmonary process of tuberculous etiology, increased by a previous immersion in cold waters (we know that the waters of Guatemalan lakes, at least those of Lake Atitlán, are quite cold).

3- The evolution of a pathological condition that had no specific treatment at the time.

Let us then settle for a cause of death.

Well, we decided for pulmonary tuberculosis, less "romantically elevated", no doubt, than death only for love but understanding that this infectious disease may very well have been accelerated by severe depression and abandonment of the struggle for life, characteristic of a loving contrariness in a personality prone to these disorders, which seems to have been that of this specific patient.

Cuban Catholic writer Perla Cartaya Cotta, a scholar of the life and work of José Martí, mentions in an article dedicated to the subject that there is a death certificate issued in the name of María García Granados —it fully coincides in dates, age and other details— by The Archdiocesan Historical Archive of Guatemala and in which it is simply said that the deceased had died "of natural death", something perfectly understandable in view of the high social position of María's family (her father, General Miguel García Granados had been President of the Republic and wasn't the only important one in the family environment) and the obvious absence of an autopsy, a very little employed procedure at that time and never used in cases that didn't have a legal connotation. The truth is that this "natural death" makes the above mentioned document something without any explanatory value and leaves us just as at the beginning, without a certain diagnosis.

Could María have survived her health condition if there had been no José Martí in her life or if she had been able to maintain a stable and normal love relationship with him?

Maybe yes, although we don't know the evolutionary degree of her previous pulmonary disease. Mortality from tuberculosis was very high at that time and the prognosis was quite bad in a large number of cases but not all died.

It could have happened, and we make it very clear that we are only speculating, that the absence of unhappiness —had Martí not existed and the problems in the girl's life— or the happiness derived from a satisfying and fulfilling love relationship might have avoided deep depression and all the negativity that comes from pathology. Again, Leonor Izquierdo, the wife of Antonio Machado, as young as María, lover and deeply loved by the poet, couldn't avoid, and we were already in the 20th century, that Pulmonary tuberculosis killed her.

Let us leave the speculations to one side and accept, since we have no more diagnostic elements, than María García Granados, the Girl of Guatemala, didn't die of cold but, indirectly, she indeed died of love.

Poema La niña de Guatemala

Quiero, a la sombra de un ala,
contar este cuento en flor:
la niña de Guatemala,
la que se murió de amor.

Eran de lirios los ramos;
y las orlas de reseda
y de jazmín; la enterramos
en una caja de seda...

Ella dio al desmemoriado
una almohadilla de olor;
él volvió, volvió casado;
ella se murió de amor.

Iban cargándola en andas
obispos y embajadores;
detrás iba el pueblo en tandas,
todo cargado de flores...

A CURSED MOVIE

On June, 1954, with a temperature of over 40 degrees Celsius under the sun, a large group of Hollywood stars, extras, cameramen, makeup artists, sound engineers, cooks, drivers and set assistants arrived to film a blockbuster movie on the remote and not easy to access zone of the desert of Utah known as Snow Canyon, a quite paradoxical name, by the way.

Besides the overwhelming heat, dust that rose in clouds when the wind blew, poisonous animals, ruthless sun, the ominous silence around the place, the monotonous and almost always expired food, the difficulties with drinking water and the unrelenting boredom, specially for people used to the lively and sleepless life of L.A., the most interesting thing of the place where its coarse and strange sand, fine sand that shone with a reddish glow at night and that everyone saw as a «singular, even beautiful, feature of the place», without wondering about the cause of the ghastly glow.

But they hadn't arrived there as explorers or tourists, they had a job to do, and the sooner they got the task that they (and some of them very handsomely, some of them not much) were paid for done, the better.

But… What movie were they going to film in such a distant and dreadful place?

Well, *The Conqueror*, a historical biopic, so to speak, of the famous Mongolian warrior Genghis Khan, a film produced by the company RKO, with money, a lot of money, from business magnate Howard Hughes and with an impressive constellation: John Wayne, Susan Hayward, Lee van Cleef, Pedro Armendariz, Agnes Moorehead, William Conrad, John Hoyt, Jeanne Gerson and around a hundred more.

Quite a big gamble. What the sponsors, director, producer or artists didn't knew, nor did anyone else in that problematic motley crew, eager from day one to end such torturous adventure, was that around 150 kilometers from that quiet and uncommon desert, across the border with the state of Nevade, in a lifeless wasteland Yucca Flat, there was NTS (Neveda Test Site) where the American military detonated around a hundred, perhaps more, atomic and hydrogen bombs between 1951 and 1992. By the time of the film we're talking about, 1954, there had been around 30 detonations, of the most primitive, dirtiest, and most pollutant kind of bombs.

They also ignored, how could they know? That the wind, due to very specific climactic conditions related to wind currents and the geographical disposition of the nearby canyons, blew constantly through the year from Yucca Flat towards Snow Canyon, carrying and depositing in the latter place residues of radioactive iodine, uranium, strontium, cobalt, and plutonium that, by mixing with the ground, make the sands glow with its ghastly and sinister reddish glow.

And so, with some or other romantic fling, not too many, more than one case of diarrhea, some falls and horse accidents, and the nocturnal enjoyment of the beauty of that place, the filming carried on.

And as everything that has a beginning has an end, and that unforgettable and problematic production —the stories of fights and intrigues are countless— came to an end, everyone got back to their homes, the feature was edited, the production house carried a huge press campaign promoting it, the film was distributed and…

And The Conqueror was a catastrophe, a true massive box

office flop, a serious economic blunder almost worth slashing your own wrists.

The film barely recouped the original investment —it took quite some time to get there, and there are people that say that it wasn't even able— and Howard Hughes, a self-centered man unable to handle defeat or owning up to his mistakes, paid from his own pockets to get it out of the movie theaters just so no one would talk about it anymore.

The critics, ruthless as always, called the film, among many and much nastier things, ridiculous, foolish, exaggerated, fantastic and completely detached from the real story, something very common in Hollywood and that's routinely overlooked, but that wasn't forgiven in the case of RKVO's blockbuster, god knows why. It was the last movie produced by Howard Hughes and it was also the last movie in which the waning RKO was involved.

But the really bad part starts now.

Eight months after the production was finished, score composed Victor Young died from an unusual brain tumor. Director Dick Powell died from a quick acting non-Hodgkin lymphoma. Pedro Armendáriz, formidable Mexican actor, killed himself when he was diagnosed with terminal kidney cancer. Versatile actress Agnes Moorehead was consumed until death by an aggressive lung carcinoma. Susan Hayward followed her to the grave due to a quick-evolving cerebral neoplasty, and Mr. Mario Michael Morrison, better known by the whole world as the rugged and hardened John Wayne, was defeated by an almost untreatable pancreatic and stomach cancer.

In the next 30 years there were 85 more deaths among the 220 actors, collaborators and technicians, all of them afflicted of tumors and different types of cancer; way above the American national average.

Marlon Brando, the first choice of RKO to play the part of Temujin (Genghis Khan), rejected the part —he was a very intuitive guy for this sort of stuff— claiming that he wasn't pleased with the script. And he died of old age.

Howard Hughes, the eccentric multi-millionaire, never suffered from cancer. He died crazy. When he was found dead —some say from hunger and thirst— in his enormous and desolate California manor,

had a reel on the projector, always playing, of his private cinema.
Which reel?
You got it right, dear reader.
The Conqueror!

What killed President Garfield?

The formal answer to the explicit question that titles this brief article is quite simple.

James Abram Garfield (1831-1881), lawyer, self-taught mathematician, congressman for nine terms, highest ranking general of the Union Army through the Civil War, hero of the battle of Shilloh and twentieth President elect of the United States of America died murdered by two gun shots, at the age of 49, by the hand of the also lawyer, pamphleteer, and "quite deranged" individual called Charles Julius Guteau (1841-1882). Putting it like that, we could end our work at this very spot, but the reality of the facts wasn't as simple as the previous paragraph might suggest. Let's see why.

By 1881, the particularly hot summer in Washington DC had very few reprieves, and for that reason President Garfield decided to spend a few days in the company of his family and some collaborators in the coast of New Jersey, The White House back then didn't have the amenities it has today, and moving towards the kindly coastal breeze of the Atlantic was a way, for those with the necessary economic resources, to distance themselves from the stifling heat and the unbearable flies and mosquitoes of the lower banks of the Potomac river, a summer plague of flying insects that wouldn't come under control until the completion of the reservoir (Tidal Basin) in 1890.

In the sunny morning of Saturday, July 2 «the trip had been announced, as was customary, in the papers of the previous day» Garfield's retinue, which included his two male sons, could be found ready for the train in the waiting room of the old railway station (the beautiful and functional station that many of us know today was inaugurated in 1907) of the capital, located at the sixth avenue. Notably absent was his wife, Lucretia, who, being afflicted with malaria, had been waiting for him for a few days in the family's chalet located in the coast town of Elberon, one of the small spa towns that had flourished in the so called Jersey Shores. Instead of travelling directly to his destination, The President, who couldn't leave aside his political duties, would make a stop at the remote Williams College, his former Alma Mater, where he'd pronounce a speech to the student body.

Garfield, an eloquent and energetic man, was having a lively talk with war secretary Robert Todd Lincoln (oldest son of President Abraham Lincoln, killed 16 years before at the Ford theater in the capital itself), secretary of state James G. Blainey, and some other associates when suddenly, elbowing his way through passengers and onlookers that filled the station, a relatively young man (40 years old) with good bearing, pretty well dressed and with shoes freshly polished right there at the station stepped in, a man who, taking a handgun out of his frock-coat, shot the President twice, almost at point blank, and from behind.

Those present there recognized that individual just by

watching him. He visited the White House almost every day, to ask, sometimes in not

very polite terms, no more and no less than to be appointed Ambassador to France. The most incredible part, at least for us, is that the Secretary of State Blaine had expelled him from his office a few days before, and Guiteau had threatened to kill both him and the President. And no one did a single thing about it. It was a different time.

Wounded in the back of his right arm, very closet o the shoulder (without touching the bone) and in the middle of his back, Garfield, perplexed, shouted: «My God, what is this!» before having to be held by his companions. The truth is that Garfield never crumbled or fell into the ground, though he was lain down momentarily in the station's floor while it was decided what to do and where to take him. At no point did the President lose conscience nor his military-like presence of mind. The gunner, with his weapon still in his hand, « a 442 Webley British Bulldog revolver with ivory grips, bought for $15 (other historians say $10), a considerable price for the time, at the O'Meara Armory, the capital itself», was detained by a policeman that was present at the time, and offered practically no resistance to arrest.

In important to note here that the Secret Service, founded by the Department of Treasury in 1865 to combat currency forgery and other related crimes, didn't start taking care of the safety of the American heads of state until after the assassination of President William McKinley, in 1901. The fact is that the wounded President was just inspected by Dr. Smith Townsend, one of the President's vacation guests, and then moved immediately by those in his company, in their private cars, to the White House, and quickly carried to his room and laid in his double bed.

Doctor Smith Townsend, close friend of Garfield from their younger days that had identified the President's wounds at the same place of the attack, as it was previously mentioned, consulted, at the request of Lincoln's son, one Dr. Bliss—no mistake, that was his name—Willard Bliss, a renowned Washingtonian surgeon and self-style expert that had tended to President Lincoln, unsuccessfully, sixteen years before. Subsequently—back then the President's office didn't have their own medical services—, other physicians eventually showed up, some called upon, some that weren't, although all of them were accepted. In the end there were twelve or thirteen doctors that treated the President, among them, besides the aforementioned two, the highly demanded then consultant surgeon of the Bellvue Hospital in New York, Frank Hamilton.

It's told that Garfield, from his bed and turning his head towards Doctor Charles Purvis, another of his physician friends present in the room asked:

"What are my chances, Purvis?" —And this one answered with a very serious face.

"One per cent, Mister President".

Overwhelming, and in this case sadly accurate answer to cheer up a gravely wounded person.

And here, in the first hours of the afternoon, begins a terrible via crucis of almost 80 days (accurately 79 days and two thirds) of President Garfield. Two and a half terrible months of untold suffering in which he lost around 100 pounds of weight (from 210-215 pounds before the assassination attempt to around 125 that he weighted when he died) and the will to live, just to inevitably die in the end, on September 19 of 1881, turned into a tattered rag of a human being, oozing pus and suffering to the extreme of tears and exhaustion. But this sad and tragic outcome deserves an explanation. Lets then scour around the details a little bit further

Two facts, both relatively justifiable, played against the President and eventually cost him his life, or at least contributed to his death. The first one was the selection of the surgeons that were supposed to treat him. All of them, or at least the ones that had a say on the matter, starting with the most prominent (and oldest) and arrogant among them, D. Willard Bliss, belonged to what was back then called the «anticontagionist school», that is, they didn't believe that pathogenic germs, bacteria, and fungi that could contaminate a wound existed. As one of them (fellow surgeon from the Belleview Hospital from New York, Alfred Loomis) declared: «They say these germs exist in the air, but I can't see these germs, therefore, I don't have reason to believe that they exist». For these gentlemen there were only environmental or bodily "miasmas" that could make people sick, and the President was obviously not exposed to them.

On the other side there were the «contagionists», younger and more open-minded, that followed the back then novel studies of European scientists Lister and Pasteur, but the involvement of these gentlemen, representatives of the true science (and of a future soon to come) was, sadly, very limited, if at all existent.

The other fateful fact, very severe on itself, was that the bullet entered through his back and didn't come out. The lead that had hurt Garfield's arm was removed early in the treatment (or came out on its own, that is not very clear), but the other bullet, the one that entered near the first lumbar vertebrae and didn't come out (until it was found during the autopsy lodged in the retropancreatic fat, a little behind and to the left of the pancreas) becoming a true obsession for the attending physicians.

Let's say, for the sake of fairness, that it was a reasonable obsession, perhaps a bit exaggerated in this particular case, since it was considered back then that lead could produce toxic reactions inside the organism that could end up poisoning and killing people. The fact that there was people that carried slugs inside their body for many years and died of something else, or of old age, was seen, and explained, as a property of that person's body in particular, that is, an exception that proves the rule.

And President Garfield's health couldn't be risked by leaving bullet inside his body, and, to be brutally honest, the credibility of those prestigious doctors, all of them prominent, couldn't be compromised by showing inability to extract a bullet from such high-ranking individual, a type of procedure that was considered fundamental. And both facts combined like a perfect storm against Garfield.

From the very first day, and several hours per day, the physicians and their helpers would turn around Garfield, place him face down, with a pillow below his stomach to raise the lower back, and they'd start poking in the small entry orifice of the bullet. At first they'd do it with a metallic probe, unsterilized, of course, later with two, widening the wound a little bit (without any kind of anesthetic, alleging that it was dangerous for the wounded as he was in the prone position), and when the anxiety increased, with tweezers and fingers, always gloveless and without washing their hands, a sanitary practice that wouldn't be in style until nearly a decade later.

As time went by, and we're talking about days, weeks, and months, the patient's fever grew, to the point of delirium and febrile convulsions, the pus oozed more and more through the aforementioned bullet wound, now turned into a far bigger hole—the irregular incisions, always open, reached towards the end a length of around 20 centimeters—, the general state of the patient was deteriorating and the desperation for not finding the «damn bullet» at last, as one of the doctors voiced in displeasure, increased to the point of obsession. Added to this was the pressure of both the public and the press, always updated of the state of the health of the patient. Some of the doctors, after hours of poking around, give up on the never-ending search, tired, frustrated, and probably hungry, and others take their place with the secret or perhaps not so secret hope that they'd be the finders of the elusive and ominous projectile.

So unbearable became the situation that Dr. Bliss made the decision of calling for the assistance, (for the benefit of the patient) of Scottish inventor (later naturalized American) Alexander Graham Bell, the alleged inventor of the telephone. The idea was that he'd use his Induction Balance, a metal detector of sorts, for the first time on Garfield's tortured back to find the bullet.

Be it because the bed where Garfield laid had a metallic frame, be it because they looked thoroughly only on the right side (on the autopsy, as pointed out before, the lead slug was found on the left side) of the back, the truth is that the operation was a failure. After thanking Graham Bell, who didn't charge anything for his effort, the search continued manually. But all efforts were in vain.

Feeding the patient, who at

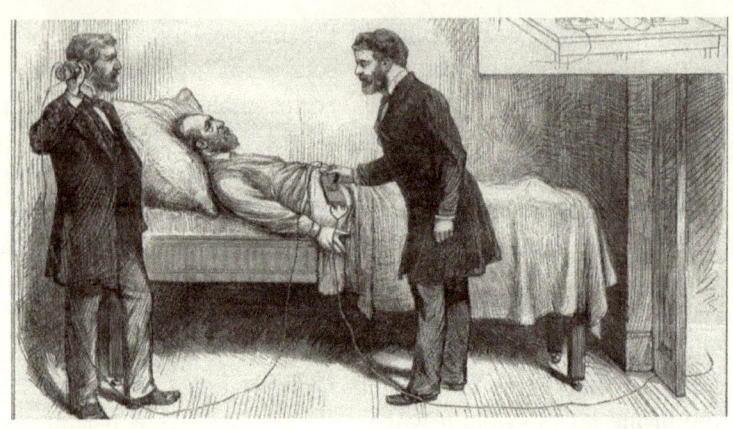

first lacked appetite and later, as the infection spread, was unable to hold anything on his stomach or even to swallow, was another challenge. They tried to solve it with enemas of both chicken and beef broth that initially seemed to work, but that ended causing irrepressible diarrhea that infected even more, if that was even possible, the open wounds nearby. The fact is that the patient was malnourished and became visibly emaciated.

On September 6, a dying Garfield was moved on a special train to the town of Elberon, New Jersey, his original destination from two and a half months before. The infection had spread through his whole organism and he was showing purulent deposits in his abdomen, lungs, throat, anus and skin, in addition to the inevitable signs of massive organ failure. But Garfield was an extraordinarily strong man and kept on holding on, in spite all odds. Against the judgment and to the frustration of his doctors, the family gave up on the search for the bullet. All that was left was prayer.

On the afternoon of September 19, Garfield, who appeared to have been in a deep coma for the last three or four days, opened up his eyes and said with a tearful tone: «this pain, this pain!» and passed away immediately thereafter. The personal odyssey of James Garfield had ended and it was time for the funeral ceremonies of the twentieth President of the United States, the second, but sadly not the last one, to be shot to death. A president, by the way, held in much higher esteem and regard by the American people of his time than what history reflects nowadays, in spite of how little time he spent on power.

The other side of the coin on this story is the killer.

Eight days before the demise of President Garfield, one of the guards from the prison where the assassin awaited trial (Lee Harvey Oswald's fate inevitably comes to mind) shot through the bars of the cell and didn't hit the prisoner's head by mere millimeters. But sergeant at arms John A. Mason, the man that tried to kill Guiteau, unlike Jack Ruby, failed at his attempt. He was demoted and sentenced to eight years of forced labor in a trial by court-martial. An unintended casualty.

The trial of Charles Julius Guiteau started on November 14, 1881 in the courthouse of the District of Columbia, and as the press of the time reflected it, it was scandalous. The defense pledged insanity and the behavior of the accused, both before the crime and during the trial, seemed to confirm the allegation.

The story of this trial — mistakes by the judge, troubles with the jury, discussions between the defendant and his attorneys, insults by the audience, intense scrutiny by the tabloid press, and other anomalies— deserves an article of its own. But among all the nonsense, a phrase by the defendant which may as well be true will be on record for posterity: «Yes, I shot him, but his doctors killed him». True or not, the jury declared him guilty and he was condemned to death. On June 30, 1882, Guiteau, well dressed and with his freshly polished shoes shining, was hanged.

During the autopsy done to the convict the doctors didn't find clear signs of syphilis, an illness that was thought could've worsened his mental issues. For the assassin's father, his son was possessed by the devil, but for some modern specialists, Guiteau was schizophrenic, an illness that wasn't understood clearly back then. The truth is that his brain was subtracted, and is preserved to this day, to our surprise, alongside Albert Einstein's own, at the Mutter Museum in Philadelphia.

Epilogue. Consultant surgeon Frank Hamilton, who participated on the President's treatment but wasn't the team leader, sent a bill to congress to the sum of $25,000 dollar

(about $600,000 adjusted to inflation) for his services.

The congress, reluctantly, approved only $5,000.

To die Young

Live fast, die Young, and leave a good-looking corpse.

Phrase often attributed to James Dean, even though it's actually a line from the film Knock on any door from director Nicholas Ray.

Dying, well yes, of course, you have to die eventually, but... when?

Mexican poet and journalist Manuel Gutiérrez Nájera, one of the pioneers of literary modernism wrote, and fully complied, since he'd die from hemophilia at the age of 35, this final verse to his poem «For Then», published shortly before his demise: To die, and young; before the treacherous time destroys the gentle crown, / when life says still —I'm yours— / Although we know well what betrays our own. Even though the verses are poetically and formally very good, the idea of dying at the prime of the physical and intellectual life —an idea that clashes directly with the natural and very human instinct of self—isn't novel on itself. A historic figure of the size of Alexander of Macedon, the Great, used to think that way and died, still very Young (33 years) around 23 centuries before Gutiérrez Nájera was born.

And he wasn't the only one: Before him, Achilles, the light-footed, and his great rival, Trojan prince Hector, died in a violent manner, while both were extremely young. Is noticeable that, unlike Achilles, a sort of demigod of living in a hurry and death foretold, Hector wanted to keep living in peace with his woman and children, even though he didn't reject death, which he knew was almost unavoidable, when the duty of defending his city was imposed onto him. So is that Patroclus, Achilles' great friend or great love, as you might prefer, killed in combat by Hector's hand, wasn't much more than a teenager, almost a child, something looked favorably by the ancient Greek, much less squeamish than us in the acceptance of homosexuality and pederasty, in this and many other cases, as a common and completely natural fact among men both in war and in peace

With 33 years of age, same as Alexander, bur with a way of seeing, facing, and explaining life diametrically different, Jesus Christ dies tortured and nailed to the cross. He dies for us and leaves us a figure that, even though in suffering, is kept perpetually young in the religious imagery, and specially, in the popular acclaim. Jesus, who, according to tradition, is the son of God and God himself, breaks the everlasting unwritten rule that sons should never bury their fathers. Perhaps because of that, and continuing once again with tradition, God, the father, resurrects him three days la-

ter. But it doesn't matter if he truly came back to life or didn't, he already showed us with his martyrdom that he could die, and die young, and last forever.

Young men die, among them many other historical figures Egyptian Pharaoh Tutankhamun (diesaround age 18 or 19), visigoth King

Reccared II (around age 20), and the almost 30,000 young men and teenager of the somewhat (or quite) mythical Children's Crusade of 1212. At age 19 French girl Joan of Arc is burned alive, and at age 31, the brave military tactician extraordinaire Cesare Borgia, son of Rodrigo Borgia (Pope Alexander VII) is killed in an ambush. Cesare Borgia was an very interesting character, who has carried with him a black that isn't completely true, which itself doesn't mean he was a saint, although very few people were in those turbulent years. So interesting is this Borgia that among other things, it's possible that he had lend his youthful face, unintentionally, to represent the face of Jesus Christ that we see in paintings, sculptures, engravings and prints of the time.

In the prime of their lives too departed Italian painter Masaccio (age 27), King Philip I of Castile, "The Handsome"(age 28), the man that drove poor Joanna the Mad insane, daughter of the Catholic Kings; Emily Brontë, author of Whutering Heights (age 30), English poets John Keats (age 26) and Percy Bysshe Shelley (age 30), Spanish writer Mariano José de Larra (age 29), tennis player and military aviator Roland Garros (age 29), famous today for the international tournament that carries his name…

But the fact is, dying young

didn't use to have the same significance centuries or millennia ago, when the population's life expectancy was statistically very low compared to what it is today. Dying at age 33 in the days of Alexander the Great, in the twenties in the times of Reccared II, or even at age 19 in the times of Joan of Arc was a pretty common event, accepted by all without much fuss. Nowadays, however, with a life expectancy that doubles and even triples the ones of those tomes, a death in the first decades of life isn't just untimely, but also shocking.

And even more startling and publicized is that death, any death, the more rich, successful, and famous the person that departs is, especially if the demise is unexpected, self-inflicted, or due to violence.

Let's review then some of the recent cases, just a few, because it's a sadly long list, so much that sometimes it seems that glory comes with a too steep price in years not lived. Although, and it's time to say it, those years not lived many times become a greater glory, one of the memory that doesn't cease that that a lot of times does nothing more than grow and being warped into a myth

The question comes to mind, and it's a legitimate question in my opinion whether luminaries such as Alexander the Gret, Joan of Arc, Blase Pascal, Mozart, Billy the Kid, María Montez, Franz Kafka, José Asunción Silva, Rodolfo Valentino, Jean Harlow, Federico García Lorca, Lupe Vélez, George Gershwin, Irene Nemirovky, Manolete, Carole Lombard, Antoine de Saint-Exupéry, John Garfield, John F. Kennedy, Sylvia Plath, Marilyn Monroe, Malcolm X, Bruce Lee, Pedro Infante, Miroslava, Selena Quintanilla, Diana of Gales, Antonio José de Sucre, José Martí, just to include some examples closet o us, all of them dead at the zenith of their human, artistic, economic, political, and historic possibilities… Had they all died from old age, what would become of their image in the eyes of the public? Well… we don't know, and that is up to each person's imagination. But let's leave the unstable future aside and concentrate on what can't be changed anymore

So, to get into the substance, let's start by remembering the sad story of "the day that music died".

The cold dusk of Tuesday, February 3 of 1959, three young men that were starting to make history in American music hire, by $36 each, a Beechcraft Bonanza, a small private plane manufactured in 1947, to avoid taking the cold, uncomfortable, and rickety bus (the three of them are tired and have a cold) that is taking them on tour through the snowy Northern-center of the United States.

They're Texas-born Buddy Holly, age 22, that following the trail of Evis Presley and Paul Anka has just recorded «It Doesn't Matter Anymore» that has already reached the first place of the nationwide hit parade; Mexican-American Ricardo Valenzuela Ryes, known by the stage name Ritchie Valens, age 17, that just had an worldwide hit with a song from Veracruz from the 17th. century and unknown author called "La Bamba"; and the also Texan Jiles Perry Richardson, known as a radio announcer by the nickname "The Big Bopper"; aged 28, who had decided, after much soul-searching, to sing professionally with the help of his own guitar, and had pushed a year before his ballad «Chantilly Lace» to the first place of the American hit parade.

The small aircraft lifts off, piloted by Roger Peterson, age 21 and with 711 hours of flight experience, without any incidents. It rises to 800 meters, turns left, dives into a dense cloud bank full of sleet and gets lost. There aren't radars that are following it, since they're on the field. Six or seven minutes later it crashes, at full dive, into a crop field. Of the plain only remain twisted debris, and the corpses of Holly, Valens, and Bopper are spread through the field. He pilot, that wasn't prepared to fly only by instruments, dies crushed against the wheel.

Between the four dead men their ages added up to 88.

The came the claims, the fights, the lawyers, their respective estates (quite meager), the press debates, and the accusations, but all of that is past history. Lets only tell one anecdote that marked, for worst, the life of good ol' Holly for many years. Before departing, Buddy Holly told one of the musicians of his bands, in jest, tgatge was mad because he didn't want those three boys getting into that frail aircraft on a night like that, and to top it off, with a pilot that looked like an Elementary School child: «I hope you freeze your ass on that bus, man!» And his friend replied "Oh Yeah? Well, I hope your fuching ol' plane crashes!"

And it did.

The list of movie actors and actresses that died during their childhoods, adolescence, or youth for many different causes is huge: Lucille Ricksen, Natalie Wood, Gerard Philipe, Matthew Garber, Sharon Tate, John Belushi, Sal Mineo, Anissa Jones, Heather O'Rourke, Dominique Dunne, James Dean, Robert Knox, Michelle Thomas, Judith Barsi, Heath Ledger, Lisa Robin Kelly, Corey Haim, Jonathan Brandis, Ashleigh Aston Moore, Soledad Miranda, Johnny Lewis, Thuy Trang, Lucy Gordon, Brad Renfro, Brandon Lee (son of Bruce, who also died young), Michael Cuccione, River Phoenix (brother of Joaquin), Cory Monteith, Skye McCole, Chris Farley, Chris Penn (brother of Sean), Dana Plato, Paul Walker and Brittany Murphy, just to name a few.

But we'd like to recount with more car, perhaps due to a personal whim, to one that died perhaps not so young: John Cazale.

Trivia Question: Who's the only actor in the history of cinema, that in all, absolutely all the productions in which he worked were nominated for Best Movie at the Academy Awards?

Answer: John Cazale.

Yes, dear reader, you got that right; John Cazale had been the only actor in the history of movies that all the movies in which he acted were nominated to win an Oscar. A feat that will be very, very hard to match.

Let's see which were those features: *The Godfather* (1972), *The Conversation* (1974), *The Godfather Part II* (1974), *Dog Day Afternoon* (1975), *The Deer Hunter* (1978), and *The Godfather Part III* (1990). When Cazale acted in his penultimate film he was dying of lung cancer and Robert DeNiro, who was like a brother to him, had to pledge his salary so Cazale could be insured and allowed to film, but he managed to do it, and the movie was a success. In his last production Cazale had been dead for twelve years, but he could appear in a cameo through archive footage

John Cazale was a master of theater, even of the more demanding shakespearean one (it was through the theater that he met Meryl Streep and Al Pacino) and one of those gems that forever change how supporting role is done for big productions. He was a nice guy, even though he didn't seem like it on screen, and a very dear friend to his friends. He was a balancing actor both on and off set, even though he usually played the part of losers.

At some point actors, directors and screenwriters like Robert DeNiro, Al Pacino, Meryl Streep (who was his partner and was with him until the end), Gene Hackman, Francis Ford Copolla, Sidney Lumet, Frank Pierson, Michael Cimino, John Savage, Christopher Walken, Steve Buscemi, Sam Rockwell and Richard Dreyfus have been asked about the actor that has had more influence on them through the years. All of them had the same answer: John Cazale. The next question they were asked was about the best actor as set parent in difficult shots. The answer, of course, John Cazale.

He had just turned 42 when he died.

Let's leave Hollywood aside and concentrate in the complicated world of music. Time to meet, with tightness in our chest, «The 27 Club».

As he dozed off, or fell asleep, probably because of hard drugs, in his house's pool, Brian Jones, guitar player and composer of The Rolling Stones drowned on July 3rd. 1969. He was 27 years old. Things like that were relatively common on those deranged years of the Vietnam War, only that a year later, in 1970, Jimi Hendrix, considered by experts to be the best guitar player in the history of pop music, would pass away, drowned in his own vomit, also at age 27. That same year, only 16 days after Hendrix, the irreverent and iconic Janis Joplin would also pass away, due to a heroine and alcohol overdose, at age 27 too. Half a year later, in July of 1971, Jim Morrison, lead singer of the rock band The Doors, dies as well, from

a heart failure of unexplained causes, probably also due to drugs and alcohol. He was... yes, dear reader, 27 years old.

What does this mean? Well... just coincidence, right?

Only that that coincidence has aroused the curiosity, or more likely morbid interest, or millions of people, and the

cases of important figures in the music business that have died at 27 years of age, before and after the original four members of the so called 27 Club have multiplied. By a lot.

Let's see some examples.

Everyone knows that Kurt Cobain, lead singer and guitarist of the rock band Nirvana, shot himself in 1994, and that formidable jazz and R&B Singer Amy Winehouse dies after drinking bottle after bottle of vodka in 2011, both, of course, at age 27.

What many don't know is that 27 is also the age at the time of the demises of Brazilian composer Alexandre Levy in 1892, American ragtime

musician in 1908, blues guitarist and composer Roberth Johnson in 1938, jazz pianist Nat Jaffe in 1945, saxophonist Bob Gordon in 1955, rhythm and blues Singer Jesse Belvin in 1960, Puerto Rican bolero singer Cheíto González in 1962, lead singer of "Spanky and Our Gang" Malcolm Hale in 1968, "Canned Heat" composer Alan Wilson in 1970, "Dyke & the Blazers" director and musician Arlester "Dyke" Christian in 1971, "Grateful Dead" member Ronald "Pigpen" McKernan in 1973, and "Bloodstone" singer Roger Lee Durham, also in 1973.

And there's where it ends, right?

No way, dear reader. In 1974, "Chase" singer Wallace Yohn kills himself in an airplane accident at, of course, age 27; "The Stooges" bassist David Michael Alexander commits suicide in 1975; singer and composer Pete Ham also kill himself that year, and band musician Gary Thain also dies on the same fateful year of 1975. And more. Composer and magnificent singer Cecilia (Evangelina Sobredo Galanes, who was and still is compared to Joan Manuel Serrat) dies in a highway accident in 1976.

In 1977 dies Helmut Kollen, keyboard player for "Triumvirat"; in 1978 Icewater Singer Chrisss Bell; in 1985 D. Boon, a guitarist and vocalist of The Minutemen is killed in a traffic crash; in '89 pianist Pete de Freitas crashes his motorcicle, and in 1993 Mia Zapata, singer of The Gifts, is murdered

Are we done?

No, no way. Kristen Pfaff, bassist of the rock band Hole dies from a heroin overdose in 1994; Richey James Edwards disappears without a trace, aged 27, of course, in 1995; keyboardist Fat Pat is murdered in 1998, and Lost Boyz Singer Freaky Tah is also murdered in 1999. Japanese pianist Kami dies from a subarachnoid hemorrhage in 1999, Spanish Singer Rodrigo Bueno is gone in 2000, American musician Sean McCabe also dies in the year 2000, Spanish singer María Serrano, vocalist of Passion Fruit dies in a plane accident in 2001, Jeremy Ward, musician from The Facto dies from a heroin overdose in 2003; also from an overdose passes away Bryan Ottoson, de American Head Charge; Sinaloa-born Mexican Valentín Elizalde is murdered in Reynosa in 2006; trumpet player Richard Turner perishes in 2011, and Austrian mezzosoprano Nicole Bogner passes away in 2012, probably due to cancer

Now we've truly finished with this atrocious list, right?

Yes, for the time being, yes. But… who knows…

Good Riddance!

Let's close this brief essay remembering the death of two famous gentlemen that, although not so young at the moment of passing away, they were still at the top of their careers (perhaps starting to fall from grace) and were, and still are, without a doubt, two icons of youth (and for the not so young) of the U.S., Latin America, and the world: American musicians Elvis Aaron Presley and Michael Joseph Jackson.

On August 16 of 1977, at some point in the early morning, close to the dawn, dies physically, at the age of 42, Elvis Presley. For the author of this essay, the person that dies inside the gigantic and extravagant bathroom, with a black glittery throne as toilet, mirrors, TV screens, phones, and a circular shower about three meters wide inside the mansion isn't Elvis Presley. And he isn't not because he escaped leaving someone else's body behind, as some claim, or because of due to one of those strange conspiracy theories so popular nowadays, no, it's because the Elvis Presley of adolescence and my youth (the one I still listen in selected records) was no longer inhabiting that obese, bloated and soft body, crammed full of sedatives, painkillers, antihistamines, antidepressants, antibiotics and anything else you can think of.

My personal Elvis Presley isn't precisely the one of Rock and Roll (actually, the so called rockabilly, that fusion of rhythm & blues and country music with upbeat tempo and acrobatic dancing), although it doesn't mean that I hadn't enjoyed him at the time, but rather the one of the perfect articulation, of the tremendous and warm voice of "Love me tender", "The wonder of you", and the deeply African-American sound of "Amazing Grace", that it's not for nothing that Elvis was raised in the deep South and virtually lived inside their churches. And of course, that superb American Trilogy, specially "The Battle Hymn of the Republic" that makes (at least

my) hairs stand.

To speak of the causes of the death of Elvis Presley is to repeat what has been already told many, many times. Uncontrolled obesity, overdose of some type of medication (important amounts of 16 different drugs were found in his body), arrhythmia, myocardial infarction (it doesn't seem to have been the cause, although he already had a severe coronary atherosclerosis), chronic constipation with fecal impaction (a possible cause of the cardiac arrhythmia due to effort), hepatic steatosis with advanced cellular damage, severe arterial hypertension for which he was already on several types of medication and a serious imbalance in his nervous system, together with chronic depression.

What killed Elvis Presley then?

For me, he died of success. The friendly and insecure young man from Tupelo couldn't handle so much. Sometimes people believe that money and fame don't kill, but yes, from time to time they do, and when they do it, they do it very early.

And the other one?

Well, the other one, Michael Jackson, was anything but young at the time of his death, but he looked the part, or wanted to look the part, which is a dangerous obsession.

Same as in Elvis Presley's case, the final hours of Michael Jackson have been extensively and morbidly related by the press and are well known by the public. A man with an enormous energy that allowed him to work as a slave on stage, on the recording studio, and on the video filming set (the bests of all history at the time, and still up there) ever since he was a child he had become frail and was literally going down in the last few years of his career.

It's evident that Jackson couldn't handle the burden that he had imposed onto him-

with 50 public performances in stadiums and great halls. As a matter of fact, he couldn't even finish one of the pre-show rehearsals. It's sad to say, but the Michael Jackson that amazed us live on stage for almost 40 years was over.

And he knew it.

Anyone that knows anything about modern music knows that the adrenaline rush that showbiz stars constantly get is enormous and has a cost. And the eternal teenager, the youthful Michael Jackson was actually fifty years old at the time of his demise.

Whas if the Propofol, an anesthetic that was poorly dispense by an irresponsible doctor? Was it the mix of benzodiazepines, sedatives, and analgesics? Was it the persistent and almost impossible to treat sleeping disorder? Was it the systemic lupus erythematosus that he had been suffering from for years? Or was it the sum of it all?

It was the sum of everything and the perennial lit flame of a privileged creative mind for music, choreography, dance, art production, and singing that burnt out too suddenly. And one morning, on June 25 of 2009, the curtain suddenly fell.

But the show must go on.

And it goes on.

Dark Deaths

Let's start, to get into subject, with a case of which I had reliable sources, even in writing, and that served my outgoing companions to alert me about the healthy doubt that every medical professional must have in front of death, especially when it's up to us to verify its causes.

While I was doing my mandatory medical service in the province of Oriente in Cuba, in the 70s, I became familiarized with the case of an old man that had died several years before, around 1964 or 1965, apparently from a brain hemorrhage; and a young and inexperienced doctor, as most of us were back then; had, after a perfunctory physical examination of the corpse, without conducting a necropsy (since it wasn't considered necessary), issued the respective death certificate validating this diagnosis.

Well then, when a family dispute over some plots of land, some money, and some animals started, all of these being inheritable properties on the old man's name, the issue escalated to the point where the police intervened and a judge ordered the corpse to be exhumed.

And yes, once the order was executed, the cerebral hemorrhage was confirmed, that must have been profuse, but not produces by an atherosclerotic vascular accident, as it was believed, but by a long nail, a rail spike, about ten centimeters long that penetrated the occipital region (with the hair covering the flat metallic head) and remained lodged, as an accusing witness, in the skull of the deceased.

That, without a doubt, had been at the time a dark death, actually a murder, even though the innocent physician that filled the initial death certificate didn't even consider the possibility of such occurrence. Why? Because in his naiveté and lack of experience, he believed what he was told: «Elderly man that had suffered for years of known and well documented diseases, among them arterial hypertension, of a good old-fashioned farming family made of well-behaved folks dedicated to hard work, a rustic but friendly and socially respectable environment, a harmonious family without apparent cracks, in summation, the ideal setting… to make a mistake and mess things up ».

And deaths like that, dark, strange, suspicious, without clear and defined reasons, or with many possible contradictory explanations that don't match, can be found all over the turbulent history of mankind.

History, and only history?

Lets choose, among many possible historical examples, a case of a dark death well known by tradition, but very poorly documented. That of Alexander the Great, perhaps the most brilliant general in all of history.

Macedonian Princes Alexander the 3rd. born in Pella on an indefinite date of the year 356 BCE., eldest son of King Philip II and Olympias of Epirus, he was educated in the military arts by his father, a though and obstinate man bent into making Alexander into a good warrior at any cost, and with the best generals at the King's service. His intellectual education was up to none other than Aristotle, How many could presume of a teacher like that? All of this, together with his personal bravery, and his natural charisma, leadership skills, and strategic and tactical acumen made him the man that conquered most of the known world at the time before turning 32 years old.

The battles of the Granicus (334

BCE), Issus (333 BCE), Gaugamela (331 BCE), the Persian Gate (330 BCE), and Hydaspes (326 BCE), all of them that he won while directing noticeably small armies (when compared to his opponents, sometimes 1 to 10) are still studied to this day in military schools all over the world.

But on top of being a great general, Alexander was a skillful politician and legislator. And also a diplomatic that knew how to (and could) sometimes use his sexual appetites aside to establish necessary alliances.

He lived on the run, against the clock, as we would say today. He had the feeling (anf the oracular predictions) that he'd die young, and during his stay on the palace of Nebuchadnezzar II, in Babylon, and about a month before turning 33 years old, Alexander fell fatally ill. His soldiers marched to see him one last time. An award and a goodbye to glory, to peering into the fathomless abyss of the future.

According to a chronicler of those times, Alexander died with the sun (around five in the afternoon, like the great bullfighters) Was he poisoned with strychnine, arsenic, or root of hellebore? (that in small doses could be also used as medicine), was he killed by West Nile fever? (an endemic viral encephalomyelitis transmitted by mosquitoes that is still ravaging many in that area to this day) Typhoid fever? Malaria? Did he die from acute leukemia or from exhaustion after a life of rampant excess? Did alcoholism have some role in his demise or was it an old arrow wound in a lung? Or maybe an acute pancreatitis caused by eating and drinking too much, or the toxins and pathogenic bacteria from the waters of the river Styx, treacherously sent from Macedon so he may never go back?

Just for the sake of coming up with theories people have even proposed that Alexander, bored of a life without peerless glory, decided to kill himself, or this one, a bit more reasonable, that tells us that his generals, too worried by his poor health, killed him so he could die as a greek hero in the fullness of his beauty. All of these and many other hypotheses could have been the causes of his demise, but the truth is that he had stacks of enemies and rivals, and many heirs to his political power and territory. Fact that he himself complicated even further by stating, when asked, that his convoluted empire would be inherited by his strongest and most purposeful general (modern historias argue this, but the truth is that previous ones repeated it like a mantra). We are, and everything points that we will remain, as we begun. We don't know what the f... killed Alexander of Macedon during his prime and at the zenith of his power. And it seems that we will remain ignorant.

Now, lets take a look at history as if it was a tale.

The mythology of King Arthur (together with Ivanhoe and Robin Hood) were an important part of my teenaged discovery of medieval literature. The wonderful city of Camelot, that castle in the hill that dazzled the Kennedys; the invincible and singing sword Excalibur, trapped in its stone, and that only a chose one, Arthur, could pull out; Lancelot, knight of the Lake; the powerful and spiritual Holy Grail, the goblet of the Last Supper, and its endless search; the gentle Sir Percival; the beautiful and dangerous fairy Morgain, and the also powerful and forever distant wizard Merlin; the Round Table, that U.N. of sorts for the errant knights; the skillful Sir Gawain; Uther Pendragon, father of Arthur; the beautiful and amorous Queen Guinevere; Sir Galahad; the mysterious and elusive isle of Avalon; Igraine, the Queen Mother; the Lady of the Lake, always ready to take back, in her pale hand that emerged from the waters, the sword Excalibur; Tristan and Iseult, and many other iconic characters related to the kind, fair, and unlikely Arthur or Britain.

Iconic characters that also touched the imaginations of artists such as William Shakespeare, J.R.R. Tolkien, Isaac Albéniz, Robert Bresson, Thomas Malory, Richard Wagner, Harold Foster, Rosalind Miles, Walt Disney, Geoffrey Chaucer, Mark Twain, Lord Tennyson, Jorge Luis Borges, Gustave Doré, John Steinbeck, T.S. Eliot, José Zorrilla, Dante Gabriel Rosetti, Thomas Mann, Chrétien de Troyes, and W.B. Yeats just to mention a few of the men of letters, musicians, composers, painters, engravers, filmmakers and poest that have sung praises at them with their works.

But... Was there really in Britain a King called Arthur? And if so, How did he die?

The discussion about the first question is not up to this bried essay. Regarding the second, most Arthurian legends say that it was his own son, Mordred, offspring of the fairy Morgain, who killed him, while Arthur killed him back, during the mythical battle of Camlann.

But let's not forget that other versions tell that Arthur, in his old age, retired with his sorrows to the Isle of Avalon, and died there many years later. But... we talk about sorrows. Yes, because Guinivere, Arthur's beloved wife, eloped with Lancelot, leaving the King heartbroken, and even worse, humiliated. And Morgain, Arthur's own half-sister and at the same time Mordred's mother, also didn't quite get along with him, all of them reasons that make Arthur's death less clear than we'd like it to be.

Accursed and forever wicked history, as a friend of mine always says. Let us leave good King Arthur be at peace, that I prefer to remember him that way, chivalrous, heroic and invincible, as he was in my teenaged readings.

After this incursion into the myth let's get back to the cold and unforgiving reality.

It's true that the champions in historical dark deaths are the rulers, politicians, legislators, and warriors; but art and culture aren't far behind, no way! Examples abound, but, since one is enough, let's give a look to the case of a genius of musical composition.

Joannes Chrysostomus Wolfgangus Theophilus Mozart, a convoluted name that is abridged globally as Amadeus Mozart, was born in the musical city of Salzburg, Austria, on the year 1756. A prodigy from childhood and undisputed genius composer, he left, after a short and inordinate life, around 600 musical plays, almost all of them masterpieces. Classic composer Joseph Hayden said of him: «Posterity won't see a talent like that in a hundred years». And he probably got it wrong, because 250 years later he's still named among the greatest. And there aren't many.

A huge talent, agreed, but also the sometimes erratic and occasionally arrogant Mozart was able to generate, he couldn't help it, an enormous amount of envy. He died at age 35, at the zenith of his creative faculties. We can only imagine what he would have done had he lived, just to say any number, twenty more years, but… What really killed Mozart? The truth is, we don't know.

Let's see what the first biographer of Mozart, Niemetscheck, a contemporary that obtrained a lot of data and documents directly from Constanze, woman and mother of the composer's children: «At his return to Vienna his illness increased visibly and caused a terrible depression. His wife was really distressed by that. One day she was walking down the Prater with him, to give him some distraction and entertainment and, while sitting, Mozart started talking about death and declared he was writing a Requiem for himself. Tears started welling up in the eyes of this sensitive man.

—I definitely feel—he continued—that I won't be around much longer: I'm sure I've been poisoned. I can't get rid of that notion —».

The fact is that Mozart got worse. The swelling spread all over

his body to the point that he could no longer turn over in bed by himself, after which nausea and vomit appeared, both of which became uncontainable; diarrhea, muscle and joint pain, accompanied by acute fever episodes in which cold vinegar compresses were used to keep him from delirium. Mozart was dying, but he was awake, and trying to finish composing his Requiem (when he worked on something he was always that obsessive) up until a few days before his demise.

The death certificate, expedited by Doctor Nicolaus Closset, physician for the Theater of the Opera, and, by the way, quite infamous professional, wrote down «miliary fever» (some sort of skin rash, something very common back then) as cause of death. But the fact is that no autopsy was performed «due to the foul odor and the abundant internal secretions of the corpse».

Leaving aside the criminal poisoning, that is, the myth (or not so much) of Salieri and other envious conspirators capable of killing Mozart, many possible causes have been examined to explain such early death: rheumatic fever (that he seemed to suffer from since childhood) with cardiac valve damage. A trichinosis produced by the pork met that the composed consumed both frequently and in abundance. A streptococcal throat infection with acute kidney failure. A case of malignant juvenile hypertension, also complicated by acute kidney failure, acute cardiac failure (edema) and an intracerebral hemorrhage to top it off, and lastly, involuntary poisoning with antimony, perfectly possible because many preparations of the time, expectorants, laxatives, emetics, cointained that toxine, and Mozart, a compulsive hypochondriac, used to drink everything that the doctors recommended. A curious fact: antimony wasn't officially declared human poison in Europe until 1866.

Another death, Mozart's, not quite clear, but let's leave poor Mozart alone, we really don't have any other option, and let's jump to the 20th. century, a dark century, if there ever was one. Let's talk a bit about the end of three men, leading figures all three of them, of totalitarian political systems that have cost millions of people their lives and cause unreasonable suffering not only to their fellow citizens, but to a large part of mankind.

Vladimir Ilich Ulianov (1870-1924) known worldwide by his alias or nom de guerre Lenin, was a communist politician and revolutionary that managed to, taking advantage of the chaos after the First World War, to take over, for both his party and himself, of the push to overthrow the rule of the Tsars in Russia and to implant a Bolshevik dictatorship in its stead.

From the wandering life of a professional revolutionary, often filled with hardships, prisons, deportations, exiles, party infighting, and economic scarcity, Lenin went to become, with proven help from the German government, into the owner of an enormous and very backwards country that started to deify him in a very short time. This being the reason why his physical ailments and maladies stopped being a medical and persona matter and became state affairs, kept under the most rigorous secrecy. Isn't that something very common, dear reader?

Clarifying the causes of the early and quite peculiar death of Vladimir Lenin, a death difficult to explain because of the stress and excess labor dedicated to « the people» and «the party», as his apologists and successors said, isn't an easy task for historians and paleopatographers.

There are four themes to resolve (the most often invoked) as etiological causes in the demise of this 53-year-old man:

• He died from tertiary syphilis, something very common at the time, but a very hard to swallow diagnosis for his hagiographers (there is proof that he had been treated for this disease since 1896).

• He dies from arsenic and potassium iodide poisoning, administered in excess by his doctors while treating the syphilis that he supposedly suffered from.

• He was murdered by Stalin, using Genrij Yagoda as a hitman for the poisoning (a man that would later be executed by Stalin himself) or using someone else, to eliminate the man that had started to question his very unorthodox management of the politburo and the central committee of the Communist Party of the Soviet Union, or, how only 8 of the 27 doctors that signed his death certificate pointed out (the other 19 would pay for their audacity with their lives),

• He died from a precocious arteriosclerosis caused by overworking and dedicating himself to think and write about the communist cause and the future of the revolution.

We will never know for certain, or in this particular case maybe we will, some day, but the story of his «heroic death» due to too much «mental work» dedicated to the working class and the communist party, that dark death, will start fading with time in the cold and timeless reality.

Iosif Vissarionovich Dzhugashvili, internationally known by his nom de guerre Joseph Stalin (1878-1953), a gray and manipulative individual, was Lenin's successor in charge of the Soviet Union.

Stalin wiped out, morally and physically, all the other men that carried out the October Revolution (Trotski, Kamenev, Zinoviev, Bujarin, Radek, Smirnov, Tomsky, Rakovski, Piatakov, Sokolnikov, Krestinski, Hungarian-born Bela Kun, and many others). He also destroyed two thirds of the ranks, the most capable ones, of the Red Army, including the top brass of the Russian armed forces: among them Marshal Tukhachevsky, Generals Yakir, Uborevich, Kork, Eldeman, Prymakov, Putna, Feldman, Gamarnik, Marshal Vasily Blyukher, who had been a couple of months before Tukhachevsky's prosecutor (poetic justice) and hundreds of other high ranking officers, one of the probable causes of the collapse of the Red Army at the start of World War Two.

Victorious at the end of World War Two, together with Churchill's England and Roosevelt's United States, Stalin's health, up to that point unscathed, starts deteriorating after 1950. The final process of Stalin's decadence coincides with the so called «Doctors' Plot», in which nine doctors, eight of whom were Jewish, were tortured (two died during the interrogations that took place at Lubyanka) and tried under the charge of providing poor care, with the intention of incapacitating or killing, to members of the politburo of the communist Party of the Soviet Union.

From that point of view, it could give the impression that the so-called plot had something to do with the dictator's deterioration, but as a matter of fact, as documents and later statements confirm, Stalin, who had started to lose his avowed mental acumen and cognitive capacity, had entered in a stage of acute paranoia that endangered, once again, everyone in his proximity and whole sectors of the Soviet population.

As a matter of fact, the arrest of the physicians is decreed by Stalin when professor V.N. Vinogradov, his personal medic, tells him that the arterial hypertension that he has suffered from for many years is out of control and that he has to diet, eliminating vodka, cognac, and Georgian wine and advises him to take a break from government duties. Another version ascribes the event to the indictment of a female doctor that writes in person to Stalin, and yet another version says that Stalin himself is the one that says that it was a female doctor who told Stalin of the alleged plot, and not his intelligence services.

Or a sum of all of them, which is the most likely.

Around four in the morning on March the first 1953, Stalin, who has been demanding NKVD chief Berla to get a detailed confession from the plotting doctors, has a dispute with him and other members of the politburo or, according to some historians, nothing of the sort ever happened and they just watched a movie and ate and drank in abundance until the early hours of the morning.

Here starts a five-day period, ending on March 5 at 10:10 p.m. in which it isn't know what happened to that man inside his dacha. The truth is that, the next day, March 6, his death is announced to the public, with a stroke listed as the reason on his death certificate, and among huge public demonstrations of sorrow and the payment of political and military honors starts the end of an era.

Eight years before, in his bunker, Adolph Hitler (1889-1945) had died. Telling his story once again seems redundant. The truth is (or seems to be) that on April 30, 1945, Hitler and the woman who had been his wife the last few hours, Eva Braun, commit suicide in the basements of the Reich's Chancellery.

Everything seems to be very clear, but... the problem lies in the fact that the Russians take hold of both of their corpses and these are never seen again. A photograph of the charred body of Hitler, delivered by the

Russians, could or could not be genuine. Nothing confirms its veracity. Another photograph of the corpse, with his signature moustache and gaunt face, before being incinerated, has been proven to be a fake.

Then… well then we must accept that Adolph Hitler killed himself from a shot to the temple using a 7.65 mm. Walther PPK pistol and his woman, Eva, did it with cyanide. And the corpse, seized by the Russian special services (SMERSH), disappeared. Nowadays we know that Stalin purposely sowed a seed of doubt about the fate of Hitler's corpse in order to manipulate information at the beginning of the Cold War, claiming that the westerners had allowed him to escape in a submarine.

But we still have no evidence of the existence, or not, of this body. Some documents declassified in the 90s assert that the bodies of Hitler and Eva Braun were burnt again and then shredded by the KGB by order of Yuri Andropov, and then thrown, in 1970, to the Biederitz River, a tributary river of the Elba.

That simple, or that dark, it's up to you.

We mentioned above the growth and development of media information, but how to understand then, looking through that lens, the (absence of) explanation over the assassination of American President John F. Kennedy (1917-1963) during the noon of november 22, 1963. No magnicide has generated more investigations, articles, books, movies and op-ed pieces than this one.

If there's a dark death, it's this man's. And we're talking, of course, of the second part of the twentieth century.

The strange deaths of actor and Hong-Kong native martial arts expert Lee Jun-fan (Bruce Lee) (1940-1973) and of American actress Norma Jean Mortenson, known worldwide by her stage name Marilyn Monroe (1926-1062), of Swedish Prime Minister Olof Palme (1927-1986), of Diana Spencer, a.k.a as Diana, Princess of Wales (Lady Di, 1961-1997), and the much more recent death of Argentinian federal prosecutor Natalio Alberto Nisman (1963-2015), although with less global media appeal than Kennedy's, the most shocking of them all by far, all enter in the category of dark deaths.

We finish this brief recount with the demise of Venezuelan military man, politician, and ruler Hugo Rafael Chávez Frías (1954-2013).

After suspending a diplomatic tour to Brazil, Ecuador, and Cuba due to a swelling in the joint of the knee (May 9, 2011), going through an incision for a pelvic abscess (June 10, 2011), a new and unexplained intervention on February 26th. 2012, the announcement, by his own mouth, of a possible successor on December 8th. 2012; the performance of a fourth surgical intervention on January 13th. 2013; a new return to Venezuela on February 18th.2013, and the official report of his death on March 5 of that same years, the full 21 months of medical progression of the Venezuelan leader leave much more doubts and suspicions than clarity.

Chavez seems to have suffered from a leiomyosarcoma on his pelvic floor, a rare malignant muscular tumor with a very poor prognosis. That's nothing more than a conjecture that can be made from the few bits of

information given from Caracas and Habana, place that the President himself chose for his treatment.

Even the actual date and place of his demise, since his corpse wasn't displayed to the public, and they remain nebulous, even today.

Another one of those dark deaths that seem to increase over the years.

One more. But not the last one.

ACERCA DEL AUTOR

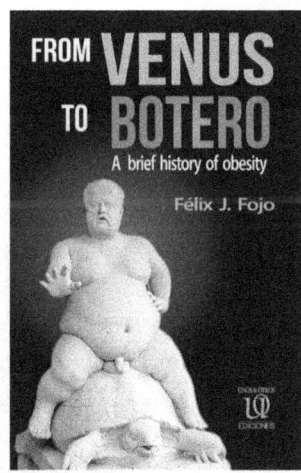

Félix J. Fojo

www.felixfojo.com

....

La Habana, Cuba. He lives in Puerto Rico

La Habana, Cuba, 1946. He is a doctor, a scientific promoter and lover of the history. Exprofesor of the chair of surgery of the university of havana. He is editor of the medical Magazine of Puerto Rico *Galenus*.

He writes for different media in EE. UU. and Europe. Among his published books: *Caos, leyes raras y otras historias de la Ciencia; Una breve historia de la obesidad; De médicos, poetas, locos... y los otros;* 2017. *Chronicles of secession; From Venus to Botero.*

OTHER TITLES

UN LIBRO DIFERENTE, POLÉMICO

LAS CULTURAS SE ENRIQUECEN, SE INTERCAMBIAN CONSTANTEMENTE, MÁS ALLÁ DE LOS CRITERIOS PERSONALES TANTO DE BABALAWOS COMO DE SANTEROS.

NELSON ABOY

www.ingramcontent.com/pod-product-compliance
Lightning Source LLC
Chambersburg PA
CBHW031409040426
42444CB00005B/491